W9-AKC-168

LYNDON B.
JOHNSON

PRESIDENTIAL ✦ LEADERS

LYNDON B. JOHNSON

DEBBIE LEVY

LERNER PUBLICATIONS COMPANY / MINNEAPOLIS

For Rick, Alex, and Ben

Copyright © 2003 by Debbie Levy

All rights reserved. International copyright secured. No part of this book may be reproduced, stored in a retrieval system, or transmitted in any form or by any means—electronic, mechanical, photocopying, recording, or otherwise—without the prior written permission of Lerner Publications Company, except for the inclusion of brief quotations in an acknowledged review.

Lerner Publications Company
A division of Lerner Publishing Group
241 First Avenue North
Minneapolis, MN 55401 U.S.A.

Website address: www.lernerbooks.com

Library of Congress Cataloging-in-Publication Data

Levy, Debbie.
    Lyndon B. Johnson / by Debbie Levy.
       p.   cm. — (Presidential leaders)
    Includes bibliographical references and index.
    ISBN: 0–8225–0097–3 (lib. bdg. : alk. paper)
    1. Johnson, Lyndon B. (Lyndon Baines), 1908–1973—Juvenile literature. 2. Presidents—United States—Biography—Juvenile literature. I. Title. II. Series.
E847 .L58   2003
973.923'092—dc21   2002000953

Manufactured in the United States of America
1 2 3 4 5 6 – JR – 08 07 06 05 04 03

CONTENTS

———————— ✧ ————————

President Lyndon B. Johnson addresses members of Congress
before signing the historic Voting Rights Act on August 6, 1965.

INTRODUCTION

CHANGING A NATION

"So we will move step by step—often painfully, but I think with clear vision—along the path toward American freedom."

—Lyndon Baines Johnson, upon enacting the Voting Rights Act of 1965

On March 15, 1965, President Lyndon Baines Johnson stood before a joint session of the U.S. House of Representatives and the Senate to make a speech. Like most politicians, President Johnson had made hundreds of speeches. Few speeches actually change a nation, but this was such a speech.

Days earlier, demonstrators had marched from Selma to Montgomery, Alabama, to support the right of African American citizens to vote. They were attacked by Alabama police. The violence began on Sunday, March 7, a day that became known as Bloody Sunday. Although the Fifteenth Amendment to the U.S. Constitution had guaranteed

Civil rights activists marching to Montgomery, Alabama, made it only six blocks before the Alabama state police attacked them on Bloody Sunday. Two weeks later, the march was completed with the protection of a court order.

blacks the right to vote since 1870, this promise meant little in the Deep South. There, blacks were often prevented from even registering to vote by white election officials and violent white mobs. In Mississippi, for example, only 6 percent of eligible black citizens were registered to vote. In Alabama the number was 20 percent throughout the state—but less than 1 percent in the city of Selma. Without the vote, African Americans were powerless to express their political preferences or to elect officials who would represent their interests.

On March 13, President Johnson had a meeting with Alabama's governor, George Wallace. As a staunch segregationist, Wallace opposed equal rights for blacks. He opposed integration, or mixing of the races, and supported the legal segregation, or separation, of the races. The president knew this. He also knew how to persuade people to cooperate with him.

"Now you got a lot of poor people down there in Alabama . . . who need jobs, a lot of people who need a future," President Johnson said. "You could do a lot for them. Now, in 1985, George, what do you want left behind? Do you want a great big marble monument that says 'George Wallace, He Built?' Or do you want a little piece of scrawny pine . . . that says 'George Wallace, He Hated?'"

A week later, Governor Wallace did not resist when President Johnson put 1,800 Alabama National Guardsmen into national service to protect the marchers. Next, President Johnson was ready to talk to Congress and the nation. "I speak tonight for the dignity of man and the destiny of democracy. . . . Every American citizen must have an equal right to vote. . . . Yet the harsh fact is that in many places in this country men and women are kept from voting simply because they are Negroes."

Speaking in his distinctive Texas twang, the president explained how African American citizens were barred from voting:

> The Negro citizen may go to register only to be told that the day is wrong, or the hour is late, or the official in charge is absent. And if he persists, and if he manages to present himself to the

> *registrar, he may be disqualified because he did*
> *not spell out his middle name or because he*
> *abbreviated a word on the application.*
>
> *And if he manages to fill out an application he*
> *is given a test. The registrar is the sole judge of*
> *whether he passes this test. He may be asked to*
> *recite the entire Constitution, or explain the most*
> *complex provisions of State law. And even a col-*
> *lege degree cannot be used to prove that he can*
> *read and write.*
>
> *For the fact is that the only way to pass these*
> *barriers is to show a white skin.*

Then Johnson reached the heart of his speech, express-
ing an unprecedented commitment to voting rights for
black citizens. "What happened in Selma," he said, "is part
of a far larger movement which reaches into every section
and State of America. It is the effort of American Negroes
to secure for themselves the full blessings of American life.
Their cause must be our cause too. Because it is not just
Negroes, but really it is all of us, who must overcome the
crippling legacy of bigotry and injustice."

The president raised his arms and looked at his audience. Millions of Americans were watching him on television. He then recited the words from the old African
American spiritual that had become the slogan of the civil
rights movement: "And we shall overcome."

By July that year, the voting rights bill that President
Johnson presented to Congress on March 15 had been
passed by both houses of Congress. On August 6, 1965,
the president signed the bill, making it the law of the land.

This president from Texas angered many white southerners, who expected a fellow southerner to support their resistance to civil rights for black people. He delighted black civil rights leaders, who had not expected a man from the South to take up their cause.

More important, Johnson's speech and the Voting Rights Act changed America. With bogus tests outlawed and violence checked by federal power, many more black citizens could register to vote. According to the U.S. Bureau of the Census, the number of African Americans registered in Mississippi rose from 22,000 in 1960 to 175,000 in 1966. In Alabama, the numbers increased from 66,000 to 250,000. By 1968, 62 percent of eligible blacks in the South were registered voters. In later years, partly as a result of increased black voter registration, thousands of African Americans were elected to political offices in the South and throughout the nation. Many people consider Lyndon Johnson's work on voting rights as nothing short of heroic.

President Johnson made history in 1965 when he challenged the nation to accept equal voting rights for African Americans. It was perhaps the highest and proudest point in his career. At the same time, however, Johnson made decisions about U.S. involvement in the war in Vietnam that would drag his presidency to its lowest points. In this way, the year 1965 mirrored the essence of his entire career, a rich mixture of highs and lows. Lyndon Johnson's life was a bumpy and exciting ride. The events that came together in 1965—so full of potential for both greatness and tragedy—were in keeping with everything that came before.

CHAPTER ONE

HILL COUNTRY ROOTS

"He wanted to be something special."
—Georgia C. Edgeworth, schoolmate of Lyndon
Baines Johnson

Lyndon Baines Johnson was born near Stonewall in the Texas Hill Country, west of the state capital of Austin. His parents, Sam Ealy Johnson Jr. and Rebekah Baines Johnson, had little money and few possessions. Their small house had no electricity, no running water, and no indoor toilets. The Hill Country was a place of poor soil, poor farms, and poor people.

Despite the modest circumstances, the Johnsons' first child seemed destined for something special from his earliest days. Hours after Johnson was born on August 27, 1908, a neighbor looked at him and predicted that he would become the governor of Texas. As a writer observed more than ninety years later, "It was the underprediction of the century."

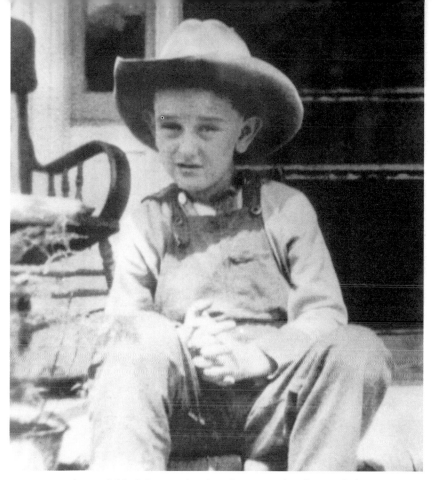

*As a child, Johnson developed a taste for the spotlight
and a knack for getting what he wanted.*

⬩

When Johnson was around nine months old, his father took him to a picnic. As Sam walked around the picnic grounds, friends and neighbors greeted him and his baby. Johnson smiled and reached his arms out to everyone he met. Eddie Hahn, a neighbor, remarked, "Sam, you've got a politician there. I've never afore seen such a friendly baby. He's a chip off the old block. I can see him running for office twenty years from now."

What did people see in young Lyndon Johnson? Some commented on his dark, shining eyes and black curly hair, inherited from his father. More important, people saw a reflection of his parents' personalities. Sam and Rebekah Johnson both possessed qualities that could foster strength and leadership.

JOHNSON'S PARENTS

By the time Johnson was born, Sam had already served two terms in the Texas legislature, from 1904 to 1908. He was known as a man who worked to pass laws that would help the poor people who elected him. Unlike many state legis-

✧ ————————————————

Lyndon's parents, Rebekah Baines and Sam Ealy Johnson Jr.

lators, Sam did not accept money from businessmen to buy votes favoring the interests of banks, electric companies, railroads, and oil companies.

Sam loved to talk politics and tell stories and jokes. The flip side of his friendly personality was a temper that sometimes flared up at home and a tendency to drink too much. Despite this, neighbors and fellow legislators liked and respected Sam.

Like Sam, Rebekah grew up in the Hill Country. She came from an educated family and lived in a fine house. Unlike Sam, who did not finish high school, Rebekah was a college graduate. She had grand ideas and ambitions. Rebekah loved to talk about art and books as much as her husband enjoyed a rousing political discussion.

After Rebekah graduated from college, she taught speech in Fredericksburg, Texas, and wrote articles for the *Blanco County Gazette*. In 1907 she interviewed Sam Johnson at the state capitol in Austin. Before autumn of that year, they were married. They moved into a farmhouse along the muddy Pedernales River, where their first child, Lyndon, was born one year later.

LIFE IN THE HILL COUNTRY

Life was hard in the Hill Country. Men struggled to coax a cotton or corn crop out of the soil. Women performed tedious, backbreaking work without the modern conveniences that had arrived in the cities. None of Rebekah's book learning helped her haul water and wood or scrub clothes. As good a legislator as he was, Sam was not so good at earning a living. He tried farming and business, but often he barely earned enough money to get by.

Poverty was widespread in Texas during Johnson's childhood, but his family scraped by. They lived in this house in Johnson City. Johnson is the boy standing next to the car.

Yet Rebekah and Sam built a life. After Lyndon, they had four more children: Rebekah in 1910, Josefa in 1912, Sam Houston in 1914, and Lucia in 1916. When Lyndon was six, the family moved a few miles east to Johnson City (named for some family ancestors), hoping to improve their living conditions. But Johnson City was not much different from the country. Although the Johnsons' house was one of the nicer ones in the town of 323 residents, it lacked indoor plumbing and electricity. One of Johnson's biographers described the town: "There was no electricity, no indoor toilets, only two houses with bathtubs and running water, no place you could buy a loaf of bread or fresh meat, and almost nothing to do or any place to go."

A NATURAL BORN LEADER

Lyndon was smart and a good reader, and he started school at age four, a year earlier than most children. As he grew older, however, he showed little interest in school. He spent his time playing, talking, and boasting.

Some people who grew up with Lyndon found him bossy and unpleasant. Others thought his strong-willed ways showed leadership. Ben Crider, a boyhood friend, recalled, "Lyndon Johnson was a natural born leader." Bob Edwards, another one of the older boys whom Lyndon befriended, said, "Lyndon was a good boy, but he was overpowering if he didn't get his own way. He had a baseball, and the rest of us didn't have one. . . . Well, Lyndon wanted to pitch. He wasn't worth a darn as a pitcher, but if we didn't let him pitch, he'd take his ball and go home. So, yeah, we'd let him pitch."

Even at an early age, Lyndon loved politics. He was captivated by talk of elections, government, and the world outside Johnson City. By the time he was ten, Lyndon was hanging out at the local barbershop, where the townspeople gathered to share news. Lyndon did not simply sit and listen to the discussions. He read the same newspapers that the adults read. He discussed, argued, and attempted to persuade them to his point of view.

CAMPAIGNING WITH SAM

Soon Lyndon got a taste of real-world politics in action. In 1918 his father ran again for election to the Texas legislature. Sam Johnson favored better roads for rural areas and more state aid for rural schools.

Sam brought his oldest son with him to campaign. Lyndon loved those times. "Families all along the way opened up their homes to us," he said later. "If it was hot outside, we were invited in for big servings of homemade

*Sam Johnson served six
terms in the Texas House of
Representatives and gave Johnson
his first glimpse of political life.*
—————————— ✧

ice cream. If it was cold we
were given hot tea...
sometimes I wished it could
go on forever."

After Sam won the elec-
tion, he took Lyndon to
Austin, the state capital, to
sit in the legislative chamber
with him. At twelve years
old, Lyndon was already six
feet tall. He shared not only
his father's height, but also
his large ears and nose,
coal-black hair, dark eyes,
and skinny build. The other
legislators all recognized Sam Johnson's son.

Lyndon resembled his father even more by adopting his
habit of standing very close to people when talking with
them, bending close in a friendly way, and putting an arm
around their shoulder. He was only a boy, but he was
already right at home in the world of adults and the world
beyond Johnson City.

CHAPTER TWO

FROM REBEL TO TEACHER

"To think that my eldest born
would turn out like this."

—Rebekah Johnson, on the wild ways
of her son Lyndon

In 1920 Sam Johnson's economic fortunes took a turn for the worse. Bad weather spoiled a cotton crop he had planned to sell to pay off his debts. Cotton prices dropped dramatically at the same time, leaving the Johnsons so poor that sometimes they did not have enough to eat. Although Sam was only forty-three, his health was poor, and he did not run for reelection to the state legislature. Rebekah, at thirty-nine, also had health problems and frequently took to her bed.

As Sam and Rebekah struggled with health and financial troubles, Johnson grew into a rebellious teenager. He frequently defied his parents and ignored their instructions to pay attention to school and chores. Instead, Johnson did the least amount of work possible. Because he was bright, he made acceptable grades, but he did not excel at school. Johnson amused himself by sneaking out of the house at night to meet friends. More than once, he took his father's car without permission—and more than once, he wrecked it. His Grandma Baines started saying, "That boy is going to end up in the penitentiary—just mark my words!"

Johnson himself had a rosier view of his future. In ninth grade, he announced to his classmates, "Someday I'm going to be president of the United States."

Despite his casual attitude toward school, Johnson graduated from Johnson City High School in 1924 at the age of fifteen. (The school only went through the eleventh grade.) Because he had started school early, Johnson was the youngest member of a class of six students. Johnson's classmates predicted that he would one day be governor of Texas.

Johnson's parents urged him to go to college. But he told his mother that he never wanted to go to school again, which bitterly disappointed her and Sam. Sam insisted that Johnson work if he refused to enroll in college. In the summer of 1924, Johnson got a job on a road crew, which he hated. After that he worked in a cotton gin, which he didn't like much better.

THE WILD BUNCH

Johnson's relationship with his father grew more strained as Johnson continued to run around with his friends at night. In November 1924, Johnson joined a group of boys who were headed to California in search of better opportunities. Knowing that his parents did not want him to go, Johnson snuck out of town when his father was away on business.

Describing his trip, Johnson said, "I washed a few cars. I hashed in a cafe. I'd say, 'Shipwreck, please.' That means scramble two eggs. Finally, I worked as an elevator operator in the Platt Building in San Bernardino, California." Johnson also worked in a cousin's law office. But that arrangement fell apart, and seventeen-year-old Johnson returned to Johnson City in the fall of 1925.

Johnson's trip to California did not turn out to be his route to a new life, but it did give him a dose of reality. Without a college education, he would have a hard time finding success. When he came back to Johnson City, the only job he could get was on a road-building crew. The work was grueling. Johnson took up with a group of young men known around town as the "wild bunch." They drank, fought, and stole dynamite from the state highway department, setting it off in the middle of the night as a prank.

By February 1927, after two freezing winters on the road crew, Johnson was tired of the aimless life. "I'm sick of working just with my hands, and I'm ready to try working with my brain," he told his parents. He was ready to go to college.

OFF TO COLLEGE

Johnson planned to enroll in Southwest Texas State Teachers College at San Marcos, not far from Johnson City. When he arrived there in the spring of 1927, he learned that his high school credits did not qualify him to attend. He had to complete a six-week "subcollege" and take exams in English and geometry. He was worried about the geometry, so several days before the test, Johnson's mother came to San Marcos to help him prepare. He earned a seventy, the lowest score a student could get and still qualify to enroll.

Johnson (right) *was on the debate team at Southwest Texas State Teachers College. He is shown here with his coach* (center) *and a team member.*

On campus, Johnson's classmates reacted to him in much the same way people had in Johnson City. Some found his personality obnoxiously bossy and overpowering, while others saw leadership qualities. Johnson's tendency to exaggerate his own abilities and achievements earned him the nickname "Bull" Johnson.

Johnson met and became close to the college president, Cecil Eugene Evans, who shared Johnson's love of politics. To the amazement of other students, Johnson easily struck up conversation with the usually distant Evans. This relationship gave Johnson access to the man with the power to hand out sought-after jobs to students. Although tuition at San Marcos was low compared to other universities, most students were poor and had to work. Evans gave Johnson a good job in the college president's office. From this perch, Johnson arranged for his friends to get jobs.

"HOW DO YOU DO, MR. JOHNSON?"

Even with the salary he received as President Evans's assistant, Johnson was short of money in the summer of 1928. To build up his funds, he took a job in Cotulla, Texas, a tiny town in the southern part of the state, along the Nueces River. He would teach school and serve as principal at Welhausen Elementary School for one year and then return to college.

Cotulla was sixty miles from the Mexican border. Welhausen was known as the "Mexican school," reflecting the nationality of its students. There were five other teachers besides Johnson, but none of them was anything like Johnson. Indeed, the Mexican school had never experienced anything like Lyndon Johnson.

A Texas-Sized Personality

Standing six feet three inches tall, with huge ears and a prominent nose, Lyndon Johnson was a large and noticeable person. He had the personality to match his physical size.

Even as a boy, Johnson liked to draw attention to himself. Students in his seventh-grade class had to sign out when they left class to use the outhouse. Most students fulfilled this requirement by writing their names in small letters on the blackboard. They did not want to draw attention to themselves. Johnson was different. He wrote his full name—LYNDON B. JOHNSON—in huge letters across the entire blackboard when he left the classroom.

As an adult, Johnson continued to want to be noticed. He wore Texas-style cowboy hats and fancy shirts, far from the usual style among powerful politicians in Washington, D.C. He named his Texas property the LBJ Ranch and wore cuff links engraved with the letters LBJ. He also saw to it that both his daughters had the initials LBJ.

Johnson's desire to excel fueled his tremendous appetite for hard work. He had a large appetite for food as well. "Lyndon was the biggest eater I ever watched," said Senator George Smathers of Florida. "He would eat two large meals and gulp them down as if he were starving. Nobody could slow him down."

Many people had a hard time accepting Johnson's outsized personality. They criticized his use of crude language and his habit of speeding around his ranch for kicks. When he served Texas barbecue to foreign dignitaries, some people were embarrassed. Critics were appalled when Johnson showed reporters the scar on his abdomen from gall bladder surgery in October 1965.

Johnson loads up his plate at a Texas-style celebration of his presidential victory in 1964. Vice President Hubert H. Humphrey is at right.

─────────────────── ✧ ───────────────────

The criticism bothered Johnson, but he could not change who he was. After he left office, LBJ observed, "The presidency has made every man who occupied it, no matter how small, bigger than he was; and no matter how big, not big enough for its demands."

Before Johnson started working at the school, teachers did the bare minimum. They taught classes and went home. They refused to supervise activities at recess. There were no after-school clubs. After witnessing a recess in the bare school yard, Johnson bought a volleyball and a softball for the students. In his role as principal, he ordered the teachers to stay with the students during recess. He started sports teams and a literary society. He coached the debate team himself. He organized spelling bees, a band, and a parent-teacher association to help with school functions.

Johnson was strict in the classroom. He required his students to greet him each morning with a song he had written:

————————— ✧ —————————

Johnson (second row, center) *with his students at Welhausen Elementary School in Cotulla, Texas*

How do you do, Mr. Johnson,
How do you do?
How do you do, Mr. Johnson,
How are you?
We'll do it if we can,
We'll stand by you to a man,
How do you do, Mr. Johnson,
How are you?

"Mr. Johnson" cared about his Cotulla students, and they knew it. He saw how poorly the white townspeople treated the darker-skinned Mexican children and their parents. Johnson wanted to show his students that through their schooling they could build a better life for themselves. He had come to accept his parents' ideas about the importance of education.

COLLEGE POLITICS

Johnson returned to San Marcos in the summer of 1929. His final year of school was extremely busy, with classes, work, and the student newspaper. Johnson also became involved in campus politics, particularly in a struggle between a club known as the Black Stars and an upstart group that called itself the White Stars.

The Black Stars were mostly football players and other athletes. They dominated student affairs and social life, with a lock on student offices—and on dates with the young women at San Marcos. Johnson had applied to get into the group, but they voted against him. A small group of less popular students formed the White Stars, and in January 1930 they decided to challenge the Black Stars' candidate in the election for senior class president. Largely at Johnson's urging, the White Stars put up a candidate of their own, Willard Deason, with the slogan, "Brains Are Just as Important as Brawn." Johnson did not seek the office himself because he knew he was too unpopular to be elected. But he worked tirelessly on Deason's behalf, appealing to students who resented the Black Stars.

Despite Johnson's hard work, Deason seemed certain to lose. On the night before the election, he was twenty votes short in a class of two hundred. Deason and others were ready to give up, but Johnson spent the evening talking to students, urging them to vote for the White Stars' candidate. It was his first time on a "campaign trail" since he had traveled the back roads of the Hill Country with his father looking for votes to send Sam to the Texas legislature. And just as Sam got the votes, so did Johnson. Deason won.

The White Stars later won control of the student council and other offices. By the time Johnson graduated from Southwest Texas State Teachers College in 1930, he had changed campus life. His aggressive methods offended many people, but he had learned how to gain power.

CHAPTER THREE

OUT IN THE WORLD

*"This skinny boy was as green
as anybody could be, but within a few months
he knew how to operate in
Washington better than some who had
been here for twenty years before him."*

—Arthur Perry, secretary to Senator
Tom Connally, on Johnson as
Congressman Kleberg's new secretary

When Johnson left San Marcos, he knew he was good at the rough-and-tumble process of politics, and he enjoyed it. In the summer of 1930, he attended a political barbecue, where he made a speech in support of a candidate for state office. He impressed some people in the audience, including Welly Hopkins, who was running for the Texas Senate. Hopkins asked Johnson to help him with his campaign.

Johnson approached the job with vigor. He traveled the Hill Country to meet voters and sing the praises of his candidate. He distributed campaign flyers and got his White Stars friends to help. He organized speaking opportunities for Hopkins. In the end, Hopkins won, thanks in part to the unexpectedly large number of votes he received in the Hill Country.

In his new role as state senator, Welly Hopkins told other legislators about the young San Marcos graduate with the amazing aptitude for politics. But while Johnson would have liked a job in state politics, neither Hopkins nor anyone else could give him one. Jobs were scarce, in government and elsewhere. The country was in the grip of the Great Depression, a period of severe economic trouble that started in October 1929 with the crash of the New York stock market. Businesses failed and farmers went bankrupt. People lost their jobs. Banks closed their doors, often depriving customers of their savings. Poverty and hunger were widespread across America.

Johnson was lucky. He got a position teaching speech and coaching the debate team at Sam Houston High School in Houston. Sam Houston High School, with 1,800 students, was twice as large as Southwest Texas State Teachers College.

As in Cotulla, Johnson was a star educator. His speech classes were popular. Students enjoyed the tall, energetic young teacher with the curly black hair. Johnson also threw himself into coaching the debate team. He selected team members from his speech classes and made them work as they had never worked before. He whipped up enthusiasm in the school for the debaters, treating them like athletes— complete with pep rallies before debating events. The team won debate after debate. Members of the Houston school board were so pleased with Johnson that—in a time of shrinking budgets and slashed teacher salaries—they voted him a one-hundred-dollar raise.

CALLED TO CONGRESS

Johnson's teaching career was as brief as it was impressive. In the fall of the new school year—November 1931—a newly elected United States congressman named Richard Kleberg telephoned him. Kleberg, like Johnson, belonged to the Democratic Party. He had just won an election to represent Texas's Fourteenth District in the U.S. Congress, and he needed a secretary. (At the time, "secretary" was the word used for a congressperson's top assistant.) Welly Hopkins had recommended Johnson for the job. Would he come to Washington, D.C., with the newest member of the U.S. House of Representatives?

A week later, Johnson and Representative Kleberg arrived by train in the nation's capital. Johnson rented a tiny room in the basement of a rather run-down residential hotel, the Dodge Hotel. His new home was within walking

———————————— ✧
In Washington, D.C., newcomers like Johnson often found inexpensive lodging at inns such as the Dodge Hotel.

distance of the U.S. Capitol and the office buildings that housed the representatives, senators, and their staffs. Johnson was now part of this elite group. At the age of twenty-three, he was in charge of running the office of a United States congressman.

In Johnson's case, this role turned out to be far more substantial than it was for many other congressional secretaries. Representative Kleberg seemed to have little interest in being a legislator. The son of extremely wealthy parents, he was one of the richest men in Texas. Once in Washington, he spent a great deal of time playing golf at an exclusive local country club. His young new secretary was left to fend for himself.

"Dearest Mother," Johnson wrote in a letter to Rebekah after he had been in Washington about a week, "I don't know when I've been so tired as I am tonight. . . . I get up at 6 o'clock and go to the office by 7:30, taking off 30 minutes sometime during the day for lunch and leave the office at six or seven depending on the correspondence. . . . Mr. Kleberg doesn't spend an hour a day there and then only signing letters. Frequently I go back at night to finish so I won't get behind. Am learning fast and doing a good job of my work."

WORKING FOR THE PEOPLE BACK HOME

This time, Johnson was not exaggerating or boasting. He quickly grasped that Representative Kleberg's success—and his own—depended on meeting the needs of the people back home. The Texans in the Fourteenth District were cotton farmers, fruit and vegetable farmers, cattle ranchers, and war veterans. When they had a problem that involved

A Texas family in the 1930s takes a break from picking cotton. As the driving force in Representative Kleberg's office, Johnson wanted farmers and other hard-working Texans to know that they had a friend in Washington.

the government, they were likely to write a letter to their representative in Congress.

Some congresspeople and their staffers simply forwarded these letters to the appropriate government agency for action—or, as the case often was, inaction. Not Johnson. He personally called the people who could help his constituents, flattering and persuading them to take favorable action. Johnson set up a strict rule that his office assistants had to follow: letters from constituents had to be answered the same day that they came in. Three times a day, the mail carrier delivered another packet of mail to Representative

Kleberg's office in Room 258 of the House Office Building. The work was never-ending.

The Great Depression was taking a terrible toll on the farmers in the Fourteenth District, as it was on millions of Americans. For the first year or so that he was in Washington, Johnson could do little to help the struggling farmers back home. President Herbert Hoover, a Republican, was unable to resolve the country's economic collapse and was unwilling to put the country in debt to do so.

THE NEW DEAL

Early in 1933, Franklin Delano Roosevelt was inaugurated as the nation's new president. As a Democrat, Roosevelt

President Franklin D. Roosevelt outlined his New Deal program in a national radio address. As a congressional secretary, Johnson worked hard to help Texans obtain New Deal benefits.

believed that the federal government should take a greater role in shoring up the economy. He established the New Deal, an extensive set of programs designed to overcome the Depression and help the nation's underprivileged citizens. Among other things, President Roosevelt—also known as FDR—got Congress to pass laws providing generous aid to farmers.

Johnson was paying attention. The very first check issued under a new program to help cotton farmers was paid to a farmer in the Fourteenth Congressional District of Texas. As more economic assistance programs were created, Johnson made sure Representative Kleberg's constituents got every benefit they could.

Johnson's talkative nature made it easy for him to meet other congressional secretaries and their bosses. He became close friends with Representative Sam Rayburn, a powerful congressman from Texas. Rayburn had served with Johnson's father in the Texas state legislature. He was a quiet, stern man who opened up to few people. But Johnson won his affection. To Representative Rayburn, who had no children, Johnson was something like a son.

LADY BIRD

While widening his circle and honing his political skills, Johnson did not neglect his personal life. On a trip back to Austin, Texas, in the autumn of 1934, a friend introduced him to Claudia Alta Taylor, known since childhood as Lady Bird, or simply Bird. Born in Karnack, Texas, she was the daughter of a successful farmer and merchant, Thomas Jefferson Taylor, and his wife, Minnie Lee Taylor, who died when Lady Bird was a young girl. Lady Bird had always

When Johnson met Lady Bird Taylor, her refined ways clashed with his bullish demeanor. He was smitten immediately.

———————————— ✧ ————————————

been rather shy and quiet, but she was also independent. She had earned two degrees from the University of Texas, one in education and the other in journalism. She had also studied shorthand and typing so that she could be prepared to go into business.

From the moment Johnson met Lady Bird he seemed crazy about her. They made a date to meet for breakfast the next morning. "I knew I'd met something remarkable," she said later, "but I didn't know quite what." Breakfast turned into an all-day outing. Johnson talked endlessly about himself, his job, ambitions, family, earnings—even how much insurance he had. And at the end of the day, he asked his date to marry him. Lady Bird replied, "You must be joking."

Johnson was not discouraged. When he returned to Washington, he wrote to Lady Bird every day and called almost as often. Then, in November 1934, Johnson drove nonstop from Washington to Karnack. This time, Lady Bird agreed to become engaged. But even that was not enough for Johnson. He wanted to get married immediately.

Johnson's powers of persuasion worked. He and Lady Bird were married on November 17, 1934, in St. Mark's Episcopal Church in San Antonio, Texas. Twelve people attended, including Lady Bird's college roommate. The ring Johnson placed on Lady Bird's finger during the ceremony had been purchased minutes earlier at a Sears, Roebuck store for $2.50. After a honeymoon in Mexico, the young married couple moved to a one-bedroom apartment in Washington, D.C.

Lady Bird Taylor was not the sort of person to be swept off her feet and talked into marriage practically overnight. Yet that is what happened. She explained later: "He was tall and gangling, and he talked quite incessantly. At first I thought he was quite a repulsive young man. Then I realized he was handsome and charming and extremely bright." Lady Bird also considered her father's reaction after she brought Johnson home for the first time: "Hmm, you've been bringing home a lot of boys," Taylor said. "This one looks like a man."

CHAPTER FOUR

RISING POLITICIAN

*"There was never a dull moment around him.
If Lyndon Johnson was there, a party would be
livelier. The moment he walked in the door, it
would take fire."*

—Abe Fortas, lawyer and future U.S. Supreme
Court associate justice

No sooner were Johnson and Lady Bird settled in Washington than Johnson became restless to make another change in his life. He could rise no further as Representative Kleberg's secretary. Johnson was twenty-six at the end of 1934—a year older than the minimum age set by the Constitution for being elected to Congress. He would have liked to become a congressman himself, but he did not want to challenge his boss for the seat in the Fourteenth District.

Then an unexpected opportunity arose. In June 1935, President Roosevelt created a new government agency, the

In the 1930s, many teenagers dropped out of school to look for jobs and lived in dangerous conditions. The NYA put students to work in safe environments such as this clerical office in Washington, D.C.

─────────────────── ✧ ───────────────────

National Youth Administration (NYA). The agency was formed to help young people make their way through the Great Depression by creating opportunities for them to work and to complete their education. Every state had its own NYA director to develop and run the programs. With help from his powerful friend Sam Rayburn, Johnson got the job of NYA director in Texas—the youngest director in the agency. In the late summer of 1935, he and Lady Bird moved back to Texas.

PUTTING YOUTH TO WORK
From the moment he set up his office in Austin, Johnson seemed driven to excel at the job, as he had as congressional secretary. The challenge before him was daunting. Tens of thousands of young Texans needed assistance. Johnson had

——————————— ✧ ———————————

Johnson (center) *sometimes visited the sites of NYA projects. His program was so successful that First Lady Eleanor Roosevelt visited him in 1936 to see how he ran it.*

to figure out how to create useful jobs, find the young people who could do them, make arrangements with schools so that students could work and study, and more. And the public, especially the business community, did not unanimously support job and aid programs such as the NYA. Many people shared the view expressed by one San Antonio business leader who told Johnson, "All these kids need to do is get out and hustle." Johnson had recently seen some children going through the trash behind a cafeteria looking for something to eat. He replied to the businessman, "Right. Last week over here I saw a couple of your local kids hustling—a boy and a girl, nine or ten. They were hustling through a garbage can in an alley."

Johnson and his staff at the Texas NYA worked seven days a week. Their efforts paid off. Thousands of young Texans were able to stay in school, thanks to the part-time jobs provided by the NYA. Thousands more who were out of school were able to earn a living. The young people built roads, parks, sidewalks, and public buildings.

The hard work also paid off personally for Johnson. Many people in Texas came to know and admire him. Politicians outside of Texas also heard of the young dynamo who put needy young people to work and helped keep them in school.

A NEW CAMPAIGN

In February 1937, the congressman who represented Texas's Tenth Congressional District died. The Tenth District included Austin, where Johnson and Lady Bird lived, as well as Johnson City. Johnson decided to quit his NYA position to run for the open seat. It was a risky move, as he was not a shoo-in for the job and eight other candidates were running in the special election. The others described Johnson, then twenty-eight, as too young to be a congressman. Sensitive to this charge, Johnson often referred to himself as "almost thirty" on the campaign trail.

Johnson's campaign focused on his promise to support President Roosevelt's New Deal programs of social and economic reform. More conservative politicians were opposed to the New Deal, believing that the government had become too involved in the nation's economy. Some also opposed Roosevelt's controversial plan to add additional justices to the U.S. Supreme Court who would vote to uphold his New Deal laws.

Johnson campaigned hard, giving more than two hundred speeches in forty-two days and traveling to every town in the district. Johnson was an up-close-and-personal campaigner. When his car reached the edge of a town, he got out and walked so he could shake hands and stop in stores. If he saw a farmer in the fields, he stopped the car and tromped over to shake hands. Johnson was at his best in informal meetings and greetings. When delivering a more formal speech, he often sounded awkward.

Saturday, April 10, 1937, was election day. Johnson anxiously awaited the outcome in an unusual place: Seton Hospital in Austin. He had been rushed there the previous Thursday night after nearly collapsing in front of a rally of four hundred people. It was appendicitis, and doctors operated immediately to remove his nearly ruptured appendix. The news on Saturday night was certainly good for Johnson's recovery: he had won the special election and would be returning to Washington as a congressman.

REPRESENTATIVE JOHNSON

Before Johnson traveled the 1,500 miles to Washington to begin his new career, he took a much shorter trip, but one of great importance. President Roosevelt came to Texas in May 1937, a few weeks after Johnson's victory, to go fishing in the Gulf of Mexico. Johnson was eager to meet the president. In turn, FDR wanted to meet the young congressman-elect who had won votes by promising to back FDR. They met in the port city of Galveston. Still weak and thin

Johnson (right) and Texas governor James Allred (center) greeted FDR (left) in Galveston. After meeting Johnson, FDR told an aide, "Now I like this boy, and you're going to help him with anything you can."

from his illness, Johnson was invited to join FDR and other political dignitaries to ride on the presidential train.

Johnson and FDR talked privately during the day. Before the end of the day, FDR gave Johnson the telephone number of Thomas Corcoran, a close assistant to the president. This connection gave Johnson unusual advantages for a freshman congressman. He also still enjoyed the favor of Representative Sam Rayburn. Because of these connections, as well as his outgoing nature, Johnson was soon well known around the capital.

Johnson made good on his campaign promise to support the president. He voted in favor of most laws and programs that FDR wanted. These included a federal agency to clean up urban slums, a minimum wage, and aid to the governments of Great Britain and France, which faced the threat of war with Nazi Germany. Johnson also made sure that his district received its share of New Deal money and assistance.

DAMS AND ELECTRICITY

Among the projects that Johnson worked on during his early years in the House of Representatives, two are especially noteworthy. He convinced the Roosevelt administration to provide tens of millions of dollars to build dams on the Lower Colorado River to control flooding. Johnson was also instrumental in bringing electricity to the Texas Hill Country. Even in the late 1930s, while much of the country enjoyed the convenience of appliances and equipment powered by electricity, many rural residents were left in the dark. In the Hill Country, people cooked and heated their homes using woodstoves, drew water from wells and streams by hand, and washed their clothes in huge vats of boiling water (which had to be heated on the woodstoves). Part of the daily routine was to lug hundreds of gallons of water to the house. Without electric pumps, there was no running water. At night, the only light was provided by kerosene lamps, which were dirty and inefficient.

Private electric companies claimed they could not profitably extend power lines to remote areas. In response, FDR set up the Rural Electrification Administration (REA) in 1935 to bring inexpensive electric power to rural areas. The Texas Hill Country was so sparsely populated, however, that at first even the REA refused to build power lines there. But in 1938 and 1939, Johnson convinced the president and other officials to bend the REA's rules. Thanks to Johnson, the lights came on in rural Texas.

No doubt Johnson's early life in homes with neither running water nor electricity influenced his efforts to bring dams and power to the Hill Country. He wanted to improve the lives of the people he represented. But there was another side to his concern. The huge projects he championed also benefited powerful businesspeople whom Johnson wanted to please. In particular, George and Herman Brown, two brothers who controlled the Brown & Root construction company in Austin, reaped millions of dollars from the dam and power projects in Texas. Johnson had become close to Herman Brown during his time in Austin as the NYA director. Alvin Wirtz, a well-known lawyer and friend of Johnson, also received large fees for performing legal work in connection with the projects. The Brown brothers and Wirtz had helped Johnson's campaign for Congress in 1937 through campaign contributions and other means.

During this period of political successes, Johnson suf-fered losses in his personal life. In late 1937, his father, Sam Ealy Johnson, suffered a fatal heart attack at age sixty. In addition, Johnson and Lady Bird wanted to start a fami-ly but were unable to fulfill that desire, as Lady Bird suf-fered several miscarriages.

WINS AND LOSSES

In 1940, at the age of thirty-two, Johnson took on a new challenge. For three short but intense weeks, Johnson worked with the Democratic Congressional Campaign Committee to help other Democrats get elected to Congress. On election day in November 1940, the Democrats held on to their majority in the House of Representatives, due in large part to Johnson's efforts. Among those who kept their House seats was Sam Rayburn, whose fellow congress-people elected him Speaker of the House, the top position in the House of Representatives.

President Roosevelt noticed Johnson's accomplishment in the 1940 election. Johnson enjoyed unusual access to and support from the White House. In April 1941, when Texas senator Morris Sheppard died of a stroke, Johnson ran in a special election for the vacant U.S. Senate seat with the backing of the president. Johnson's campaign motto was "Franklin D and Lyndon B!," printed on thou-sands of bumper stickers and other items. As in 1937, the central theme of Johnson's campaign was his support of President Roosevelt's agenda. Most important, Johnson vowed to back FDR's decisions in the widening world war.

Despite White House support, Johnson experienced his first major political loss. Out of a large slate of candidates,

W. Lee O'Daniel was a Texas businessman and radio personality whose popularity propelled him to the governor's seat and then to the Senate.

─────────────── ◇ ───────────────

one was the governor of Texas, W. Lee O'Daniel, known as "Pappy." Some observers argued that O'Daniel got thousands of votes dishonestly, but in the end he had 175,590 votes to Johnson's 174,279. Johnson was not going to the Senate in 1941.

CHAPTER FIVE

"LANDSLIDE LYNDON"

*"Hello, down there! This is your friend, Lyndon
Johnson, your candidate for the United States
Senate. I hope you'll vote for me on Primary
Day. And bring along your relatives to vote, too."*
—Candidate Johnson addressing potential voters
by microphone from his campaign helicopter

Johnson was crushed by his defeat in the Senate race.
He spoke about leaving politics and going home to Texas.
But Johnson did not quit. On December 7, 1941, Japanese
forces attacked the U.S. port of Pearl Harbor in Hawaii.
The United States entered World War II, declaring war on
Japan and on Nazi Germany. On December 8, Johnson
applied to be placed on active duty with the U.S. Navy. A
short time later, he left for assignments in California. Lady
Bird ran his congressional office in his absence.

Johnson was soon restless doing paperwork on the sidelines of the war. He wanted to go overseas. FDR agreed to

Johnson's crew in New Guinea prepares for a raid on Japanese targets. Some historians say that Johnson felt combat service was necessary to advance his political career, but he also appeared to want to serve in the war effort.

─────────────── ✧ ───────────────

send him to the South Pacific as part of a three-man team to survey equipment and manpower in the war against Japan. Johnson visited China, the Fiji Islands, New Caledonia, New Zealand, and Australia, taking stock of American supplies and morale. But Johnson sought more— he wanted to see battle. And so, on June 9, 1942, he joined an air combat mission to attack Japanese positions in northwest New Guinea.

For Johnson's participation in the raid, General Douglas MacArthur personally awarded him a Silver Star medal for gallantry in action. At first Johnson seemed to have doubts about whether he deserved the medal. Other participants in the raid later gave conflicting accounts of whether Johnson's plane actually came under fire. But he did accept the honor. Shortly afterward, FDR directed all congressmen in the military to return to work in Congress. Johnson's wartime service was over.

FAMILY MATTERS

Back in Washington, Johnson worked on legislation aimed at strengthening the U.S. armed forces. Politically, he was restless again. Aware of the fact that the men in his family tended to die young—and that his father had suffered heart disease as a young man—Johnson was anxious to achieve things quickly.

If he felt stagnant in his career, at home he had reason to feel revitalized. After years of trying to start a family, on March 19, 1944, Lady Bird gave birth to a daughter. The overjoyed parents named her Lynda Bird.

At around this time, Johnson and his wife also made an important financial decision. Using money that Lady Bird had inherited from her father, they bought a radio station in Austin, Texas. The station prospered, and the Johnsons' holdings later expanded into television and other enterprises. Their increasing prosperity was a mixed blessing, however. Throughout Johnson's career, he faced questions about whether government officials in charge of regulating radio and television gave special treatment to the Johnsons' businesses.

Franklin Roosevelt died on April 12, 1945, shortly before the end of World War II. Johnson felt that his chances of advancing in politics were diminished without the support of the president. FDR's successor, President

Harry S. Truman, had no reason to favor Johnson. By 1947, after a decade as a congressman, Johnson felt stuck. "He was thirty-nine years old," said Horace Busby, an aide. "He believed, and he believed it really quite sincerely. . . that when a man reached forty, it was all over. And he was going to be forty in 1948. And there was no bill ever passed by Congress that bore his name; [and he felt that] he had done very little in life."

Johnson's family life provided some of the light and joy missing from his work life. In 1947 Lady Bird gave birth to another girl, named Lucy Baines. Now there were four Johnsons with the initials LBJ. Thrilled as Lady Bird and

———————————— ✧ ————————————

Johnson enjoyed the love and support of the other three LBJs
(left to right): *Lynda Bird, Lady Bird, and Lucy Baines.*

Johnson were to have children, their busy lives often prevented them from spending time with Lynda and Lucy. The girls sometimes fought to get their parents' attention. As Lucy later said, "I wanted a normal life. I wanted a father who left the office and came home at a reasonable hour and a mother who made cookies. That wasn't what we had."

ANOTHER RUN FOR THE SENATE

In 1948 Johnson was ready to try once more for the Senate seat that had eluded him seven years earlier. This time Johnson faced a formidable new opponent in the Democratic primary election: Coke Stevenson, a popular

Johnson campaigned aggressively for a seat in the Senate—even renting a helicopter. He knew that the Senate was a good place to develop the experience that could lead to national prominence.

former governor of Texas. In this campaign, in contrast to his earlier runs for office, Johnson no longer stressed his devotion to the New Deal. FDR was dead, and Texans were generally more conservative than they had been in the past—meaning they wanted less government interference in their lives.

Johnson's views on foreign policy were also in line with the more conservative atmosphere in Texas and the nation. He supported a strong military, even in peacetime. Although World War II had ended in 1945, the United States and other democracies feared a new threat: Communism. The Soviet Union had adopted this political and economic system in 1917. The Communist Party controlled the government, the military, and the economy, leaving little room for individual freedoms. Many Americans worried that the Soviet Union intended to extend the reach of Communism in Eastern Europe and elsewhere. Johnson backed the new foreign policy of "containment," formulated by President Truman, in which the United States was committed to limiting the worldwide power of Communism.

Johnson badly wanted to win the 1948 election—he told some friends that he would retire from politics if he lost. So he did not rely only on tried and true methods of campaigning. Johnson amazed and amused the people of Texas with his "Johnson City Flying Windmill." The Flying Windmill was a helicopter that carried Johnson from town to town throughout the vast state. Helicopters were still a novelty in those days, and few Texans had ever seen one. People thronged to see the strange flying machine—and of course, the man it carried, Lyndon Johnson.

BOX 13

Election day for the Democratic primary was July 24, 1948. Of the eleven Democratic candidates running for the Senate seat, no one received a majority. Johnson got 34 percent of the total, and Coke Stevenson won 40 percent. A runoff election was held a month later to decide between these two top vote getters. The final count, tabulated six days after the August 28 election, was 494,191 votes for Johnson, and 494,104 votes for Stevenson. The Texas Election Bureau declared Johnson the winner, by a margin of a scant 87 votes out of more than 900,000.

Coke Stevenson was outraged. He and his supporters claimed that Johnson obtained his winning edge by cheating—among other things, by adding fake votes for Johnson to the totals from Jim Wells County in southern Texas. The alleged fraudulent votes were contained in a ballot box that soon became famous throughout Texas—Box 13. Stevenson challenged Johnson's victory in a court case that went all the way to the U.S. Supreme Court. But the Supreme Court turned down Stevenson's appeals. Johnson went on to win the general election in November against the Republican candidate.

The close election won Johnson an ironic nickname: "Landslide Lyndon." But it also produced the result he wanted. He was now Senator Lyndon Johnson.

CHAPTER SIX

SENATOR JOHNSON

*"He made the Senate function better
than anyone. He pushed things around;
he got things done."*

—Senator William Fulbright, on Johnson as Senate
Majority Leader

Lyndon Johnson had never lacked energy and ambition, and he lived up to his potential in his new job. He mastered the rules and customs of the Senate as he had in the House. Johnson continued to work hard and to drive the people who worked for him to give their best effort. Many people were inspired and charmed by the new senator. He could be the life of a party, telling jokes and doing impersonations. Johnson was at his best in a relaxed setting, where he could relate to people one on one. In a more formal arena, he was still in some ways the country boy from Texas—awkward and speaking with a pronounced Texas twang.

RACE RELATIONS

Johnson kept up his friendship with Speaker of the House Sam Rayburn. In the Senate, Johnson developed a similar friendship with another powerful older man, Senator Richard Russell of Georgia. Senator Russell was famous for his extensive knowledge of history and politics. Like Johnson, he was a friend to the farmer. But Senator Russell was also unapologetically bigoted. He was a firm defender of the South's legalized system of race discrimination and segregation, known as "Jim Crow." Jim Crow laws prevented

———————————— ✧ ————————————

The South's system of segregation extended to public transportation as well as other services. Buses and railroad cars had sections in the back marked "Colored."

African Americans from enjoying equal treatment with whites in nearly every aspect of life, from schooling to dining out to voting. Across the South, public drinking fountains, schools, restaurants, and hotels were "whites-only" facilities. Southern election officials regularly turned African Americans away from voting booths.

It was not clear where Johnson stood on these issues as he started his Senate career. He had not taken a stand against the Jim Crow system. Yet he was not a die-hard segregationist like Senator Russell. Johnson declined to join the Southern Caucus against civil rights in the Senate. Also, his friendships with southern segregationists did not prevent him from making alliances with people who held different views, including civil rights advocates such as Senator Hubert H. Humphrey of Minnesota.

LEADING THE DEMOCRATS

In 1951 Johnson's fellow Democratic senators elected him their party whip. Officially, the whip's main job was to make sure Democratic senators were present in the Senate chamber for important votes. For Johnson, the post was an opportunity to develop his leadership and negotiating skills. It also led to his election as Democratic Party leader in 1953. By then, Republican Dwight Eisenhower was president, and Republicans held more seats in the Senate than Democrats did. This meant that Johnson was the Senate's Minority Leader. The Majority Leader was a post held by a Republican. Nevertheless, his influence in Washington was significant and growing.

Johnson's six-year term as a senator was up in 1954, and he campaigned hard to win reelection. He visited every congressional district in Texas, giving as many as fifteen speeches a day. He shook thousands of hands. Johnson also campaigned for other Democrats. The efforts produced results for him and for his party. Johnson was reelected, and the Democrats regained a majority in the Senate. When the legislators returned to work in January 1955, they appointed Johnson Majority Leader. At forty-six years old, he was the youngest person ever to hold the position.

If ever a man and a job seemed made for one another, they were Lyndon Johnson and the position of Senate Majority Leader. The Majority Leader guides the majority party's leadership of the Senate. He or she must appeal to senators to work in the interests of the nation and the party as a whole, while understanding that senators also serve their own states' interests. As Majority Leader, Johnson controlled who got to serve on which committee, when a bill would go to the Senate floor for debate, and when it would be put to a vote.

Before long Johnson was a master of the legislative process. "He was always keeping head counts," said Senator Hubert Humphrey. "Johnson said the first lesson of politics is to be able to count. . . . He never, ever permitted a vote to take place if he could help it until he thought we had maximum strength on our side and, hopefully, some reduction of strength on the other." Johnson also mastered the personal side of politics. According to Humphrey, "He knew a great deal about every senator and his family. He knew about the senator and the senator's friends, and he always knew where a senator was. I mean you could be out of town, anyplace, and he would know where you were. He would find ways and means of discovering where you were.

And if he needed you he would be after you, and he'd maybe sometimes get a plane to send out after you."

Johnson did not work only with Democrats. He often supported President Eisenhower's proposals, especially on foreign affairs, and he worked closely with the Republican administration to pass laws. Under Johnson's leadership, Congress increased the minimum wage and passed a law providing public housing for poor people.

PHYSICAL BREAKDOWN

As Johnson's political power rose, his physical health suffered. His workdays were long and hurried. Dinner was often late at night, with people he brought home from work. Johnson liked rich food—in great quantities. Southern-style chicken-fried steak and Mexican dishes were favorites, as were desserts such as puddings, German chocolate cake, and coconut cream pie. He drank Scotch whiskey and smoked several packs of cigarettes every day. Reading late into the night, he would sometimes call assistants at two or three A.M. or telephone a senator before dawn. Johnson grew tired, and people noticed that he was irritable.

Johnson's long hours, poor eating habits, drinking, and smoking took their toll in the summer of 1955. After six months of being Majority Leader, he suffered a serious heart attack over the Fourth of July weekend. The day after the attack, doctors at Bethesda Naval Hospital in Bethesda, Maryland, put their patient's chance of survival at only 50 percent. By the fourth day, however, Johnson was improving. He remained in the hospital for a month. Afterward, he went to Stonewall, Texas, to the ranch he and Lady Bird had bought a few years earlier on the Pedernales River.

THE JOHNSON TREATMENT

Through a mixture of flattery, friendship, favor trading, threats, and his own homespun wheedling, Johnson often got people to do what he wanted. Using these skills, he became an extraordinarily productive Senate Majority Leader.

Johnson's approach was widely known as "the Treatment." He would throw his arm around a senator's shoulder and tell the senator how important he or she was to the success of the issue at hand. He would pay extravagant compliments. He would warn of the consequences of refusing to go along. He would try to make the other person feel that he or she would be selfish to turn Johnson down. He would pressure the senator's spouse or, if he should get them on the telephone, the senator's children.

The Treatment was not something Johnson thought up one day and decided to do. It was the natural outgrowth of his total focus on politics. One journalist observed in 1951 that the young senator was "entirely preoccupied with the science of politics. He refused to be trapped into thinking about or discussing sports, literature, the stage, the movies, or anything else in the world of recreation." Representative Carl Albert of Oklahoma explained that Johnson "never dropped his intensity. He was one of those salesmen that just never quit pushing. He wanted it done, and he wanted it all done, and he wanted more done. He was a great salesman. His greatest talent was his absolute tenacity. He never, never relaxed."

After he became president, Johnson adapted his unique style of persuasion to his new job. Domestic policy aide Joseph Califano explained how the president used the Treatment: "[We] were swimming, and we stopped near the deep end," Califano said. "He was poking me in the shoulder for emphasis as he talked. 'I want to straighten out the transportation mess in this country,' he said. 'Next, I want to

Johnson (left) *puts the Treatment to use during a campaign.*

———————————— ✧ ————————————

rebuild American cities. Third, I want a fair-housing bill.' He asked me if I would help him do these things. Breathless from treading water, I told him I would. I didn't find out until later that Johnson had brought me to a spot where he could stand but I had to tread water."

During the fall and part of the winter, he recuperated through rest, dieting, and exercise. Still, the Majority Leader remained very much in charge politically. He worked from the ranch, where senators and other politicians visited frequently.

A STAND AGAINST SEGREGATION

Johnson returned to the Senate on January 3, 1956, forty pounds lighter from his careful new diet and ready to get back to work. He continued his strategy of cooperating with President Eisenhower on many issues, especially foreign policy. One newspaper columnist suggested that perhaps Majority Leader Johnson was more powerful than the president of the United States, "because he [Johnson] loves to exercise power and President Eisenhower does not."

Johnson also loved to exercise leadership. In 1956 he was one of only three southern senators who refused to sign the so-called Southern Manifesto. The manifesto declared that southern states would not permit black children to go to school with whites. This declaration was in open defiance of the U.S. Supreme Court's ruling in the 1954 case *Brown v. Board of Education of Topeka, Kansas.* In that case, the Court had ruled that the "separate but equal" education provided for black children in the South was unconstitutional. The Court said that segregated schools violated the civil rights guaranteed to black citizens under the Fourteenth Amendment to the U.S. Constitution.

Johnson had come to realize that segregation could tear apart the nation. While other southern leaders vowed to fight all efforts to dismantle the South's segregated society, Johnson took a different path. In 1957 he helped the

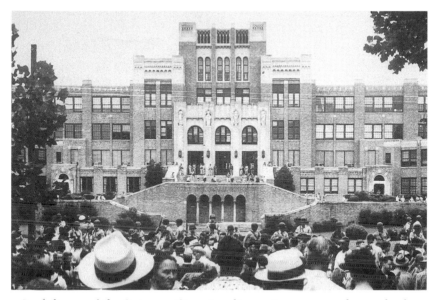

In defiance of the Supreme Court's ruling to integrate southern schools, Arkansas's governor Orval Faubus ordered the National Guard to keep black students from entering Little Rock's Central High in 1957.

Senate pass a civil rights law proposed by the Eisenhower administration. The bill authorized the U.S. Department of Justice to get involved in some types of civil rights lawsuits. It created a commission to study the nation's civil rights problems and to recommend further legislation.

The Civil Rights Act of 1957 did not do much to improve the lives of black Americans. It did not address the problem of continued segregation in schools and elsewhere. Roy Wilkins, leader of the nation's most prominent civil rights organization, the National Association for the Advancement of Colored People (NAACP), called it "soup made from the shadow of a thin chicken that had starved to death." But it was the first civil rights law of any kind since 1875. As Wilkins also said, "If you are digging a ditch with a teaspoon, and a man comes along and offers you a spade, there is something wrong with your head if you don't take it because he didn't offer you a bulldozer."

Johnson may have embraced the cause of civil rights gradually, but he approached another pet project, American space exploration, without hesitation. He was an early and enthusiastic supporter of the U.S. space program. In 1958 he played an important role in the passage of the National Aeronautics and Space Act. The law created NASA—the National Aeronautics and Space Administration—to advance the nation's knowledge of space flight and exploration and related issues.

In September 1958, Johnson suffered a difficult personal loss when his mother, Rebekah, died of cancer. She was seventy-eight years old. Johnson had just turned fifty. Rebekah Johnson's death, as well as the memory of his own heart attack three years earlier, had a major effect on her son. He became depressed and talked again of quitting politics. But by 1960, he lifted himself out of his doldrums and decided to reach for his highest goal yet: the presidency.

CHAPTER SEVEN

FROM VICE PRESIDENT TO PRESIDENT

"I detested every minute of it."
—Lyndon Johnson, on being vice president

Johnson set out to run for the presidency in 1960. But his campaign to win the Democratic Party's nomination lacked his trademark energy. He entered the race late and made few campaign appearances. Johnson seemed to think that his work in the Senate was evidence of his strong leadership qualities. He tried to portray himself as a national figure, but with his thick accent and Texas style, many people saw him strictly as a southerner. At the Democratic National Convention in Los Angeles in July 1960, popular senator John F. Kennedy of Massachusetts won the nomination as the Democratic presidential candidate. Johnson came in second place.

To many people's surprise, Kennedy wanted Johnson to run with him as the vice presidential candidate. This was

surprising because many of Kennedy's own advisers did not
like Johnson. But Kennedy seemed to think Johnson was
the best person for the job. Kennedy told journalist Hugh
Sidey, "Lyndon would be the best man I could get to run
with me. He's a Texan, a Southerner, he knows Congress,
Washington, and he has the ability to be President. But I'm
convinced he wouldn't take it. He'd be more powerful stay-
ing as Majority Leader."

The next morning, Kennedy offered Johnson the vice
presidential spot. Johnson accepted. Opposing the
Democratic ticket of JFK and LBJ—both men were often

———————————————— ✧ ————————————————

*Some advisers to John F. Kennedy, seen here campaigning with his wife,
Jacqueline, in New York City, didn't like Johnson's unrefined Texas ways.*

referred to by their initials—were the Republican candidates, Vice President Richard M. Nixon for president and Ambassador Henry Cabot Lodge Jr. for vice president.

CAMPAIGNING WITH JFK

Johnson campaigned hard in the South, where many Democrats viewed the "Yankee" Kennedy with suspicion. He openly addressed some voters' concerns about Kennedy being a Catholic. No member of the Roman Catholic religion had ever been elected president, and Catholics encountered prejudice in many parts of the nation. On September 9, 1960, 150 Protestant clergy gathered in Washington, D.C., and issued a statement warning that Kennedy would follow the foreign policy of the Catholic pope. In speeches Johnson made the next month throughout the South, he appealed to voters not to let religion become an issue in the campaign. He included the story of Kennedy's older brother, Joseph Kennedy Jr., who crashed in an airplane during World War II with a copilot from Texas. "I'm sure that they didn't ask each other what church they went to," Johnson told his audience. "They both died for their country."

JFK and LBJ won the election in November by a small margin of votes. Many political observers believed that Johnson deserved credit for the win. Without him, they said, Nixon probably would have won Texas and North and South Carolina.

The victory was bittersweet for Johnson, however. He was well aware that the vice presidency could be a fast route to political powerlessness. Despite the title, the vice president is not necessarily the second most powerful person in the nation. The president is under no obligation to share power with the vice president. Presidents are more likely to turn to familiar and trusted advisers for assistance. Perhaps that is why some observers thought that Johnson appeared unhappy after he and Kennedy were declared the winners.

VICE PRESIDENT JOHNSON

As Vice President Johnson took the oath of office on Inauguration Day, January 20, 1961, he may have wished he were being sworn in as president. Still, he applied himself to his new position with dedication. He became chairman of the president's Committee on Equal Employment Opportunity, which promoted jobs for and fought discrimination against African Americans. President Kennedy also appointed Johnson chair of the National Aeronautics and Space Council, which had been created by the 1958 Space Act. And Johnson traveled widely, representing his country and the president in dozens of foreign nations.

Johnson worked hard at all of his assignments. Journalist Drew Pearson said, "Mr. Johnson as Vice President did a terrific job in many respects, far beyond what a normal Vice President could do. First, as Chairman of the Equal Opportunities Committee he called in the big defense contractors and said, 'Now look, you are going to employ Negroes, or you will not get more defense contracts from the Defense Department....' [This] took courage and it took some initiative."

Perhaps the most eventful parts of Johnson's vice presidency were his trips abroad. He had rarely traveled outside the United States before, he spoke no foreign languages, and he had little knowledge of foreign cultures. But he

During a trip to Pakistan, Johnson greets a camel driver.
—————————————— ✧

knew how to meet people and how to work a crowd. Visiting nations as far away as Senegal and India, Johnson greeted the crowds of people who came to see him, shaking hands as if he were running for office. In poor nations, he talked about his own poverty as a boy. In Kayar, a small fishing village in the African nation of Senegal, Johnson tasted raw fish, kissed babies, and shook hands all around—despite the U.S. ambassador's warning not to go out among the people because of the threat of disease.

CONTAINING COMMUNISM IN VIETNAM

Although Johnson's foreign trips were mainly about spreading goodwill, some had foreign policy significance as well. In May 1961, he visited South Vietnam. The nation of Vietnam was divided into the North, which was ruled by a Communist government, and the South. South Vietnam's government was anti-Communist but unstable, weak, and corrupt. Communist guerrillas, or fighters, lived in the South but received assistance from the North to stage

attacks on the South Vietnamese government. These guerrillas were known as the Viet Cong. The Communist governments of North Vietnam, the People's Republic of
China, and the Soviet Union helped the Viet Cong.

As part of its policy of fighting the spread of
Communism, the United States had been helping South
Vietnam since the mid-1950s. First the United States sent
military aid, then military advisers. On his trip, Johnson reaf-
firmed that the United States would not withdraw from
Southeast Asia. He also urged South Vietnam's president, Ngo
Dinh Diem, to improve the living conditions of his people.

Johnson's report to President Kennedy emphasized the
importance of Vietnam to American interests. This conclu-
sion was in keeping with the prevailing view of many foreign policy experts, who feared that Communist
governments would take over the countries of Southeast
Asia one after another. This view was called the "domino
theory," based on the notion that the countries would fall
like dominoes into Communist hands, posing a danger to
democratic governments around the world.

DARK DAYS

Despite Johnson's activities as vice president, he grew
dissatisfied with the job. He had hoped to do more—in
particular, to maintain a strong hand in the Senate and
House, building on his years as Senate Majority Leader. "I
think he had hoped that he could be sort of the Majority
Leader and still be Vice President," one journalist commented. But that did not happen. By November 1963,
Johnson hinted to friends that he might not want to run
for vice president again in November 1964, when JFK

would be up for reelection. Johnson was not thinking of challenging Kennedy. But some friends thought he might leave politics.

Any such plans disappeared on November 22, 1963. The president and vice president were in Texas with their wives, meeting with officials of the Texas Democratic Party. First they visited San Antonio, then Houston, then Fort Worth. Everywhere, they were greeted by welcoming crowds. Late in the morning of November 22, they flew from Fort Worth to Dallas.

A motorcade of political figures made its way from the airport to the city, where President Kennedy was scheduled to speak at the Dallas Trade Mart. President Kennedy rode in a large convertible limousine with Mrs. Kennedy and Texas Governor John Connally and his wife. Vice president Johnson and Lady Bird rode in a car behind them with Texas Senator Ralph Yarborough. The day was clear and beautiful and the cars' tops were down so the passengers could ride in the open air. When the motorcade reached downtown Dallas, it met cheering crowds.

Then, as President Kennedy's car turned a corner, a loud noise rang out, followed by two more. The Secret Service agent riding with Vice President Johnson saw that President Kennedy had slumped in his seat. "Get down!" the agent shouted at the vice president. "Get down!" He grabbed Johnson's shoulder, pushed him down, and threw his own body on top of the vice president's.

In minutes, the cars were at Parkland Hospital. Governor Connally was wounded and bloodied. President Kennedy lay on his face in his car, pools of blood around him. He was whisked to the emergency room. Secret

Service agents hurried Vice President and Mrs. Johnson into a room to await news of the president's condition. Soon a priest arrived to see the wounded president, and at 1:20 P.M., a Secret Service agent came into the room where the Johnsons were waiting anxiously. President Kennedy was dead. Under the rules of the U.S. Constitution, the presidency now fell to Lyndon Johnson.

SWORN IN

At the time, no one knew who had killed President Kennedy. Secret Service officials and others feared that the shooting might have been part of an international plot against the U.S. government. Because of concerns that the vice president and other members of the government were at risk, Johnson and his wife returned to the Dallas airport under heavy guard in an unmarked car. There, they boarded the presidential plane, *Air Force One*. Johnson called the dead president's brother, U.S. Attorney General Robert Kennedy, who was in Washington, D.C. They decided that Johnson should take the oath of office as soon as possible, before flying back to the capital.

Soon Dallas Judge Sarah Hughes boarded the plane. Mrs. Kennedy also arrived, accompanying the coffin that held her husband's body. Still wearing her bloodstained pink suit, just two hours after her husband's assassination, she appeared to be in shock. But she wanted to be present for the swearing-in. Using a slip of paper on which an aide had hastily scribbled the oath of office, Judge Hughes swore in Lyndon Baines Johnson as the thirty-sixth president of the United States. With Lady Bird on one side and Mrs. Kennedy on the other, Johnson repeated the words of the

Lyndon Johnson takes the oath of office to become the president of the United States in the cabin of the presidential plane. On his left is Jacqueline Kennedy and at his right is Lady Bird.

oath: "I do solemnly swear that I will faithfully execute the office of president of the United States, and will to the best of my ability preserve, protect, and defend the Constitution of the United States."

Then *Air Force One* took off. Only a few hours had passed since Kennedy and Johnson had arrived in Dallas. One president was dead. Another had reached the goal he had been working toward his entire life. But President Lyndon Johnson had never wanted to reach his goal this way.

Lyndon Johnson's first official portrait as president of the United States was taken on November 29, 1963, one week after the assassination of John F. Kennedy.

CHAPTER EIGHT

TAKING OVER

*"An assassin's bullet has thrust upon me the
awesome burden of the Presidency. I am here
today to say I need your help; I cannot bear
this burden alone. I need the help of all
Americans, and all America."*
—President Johnson addressing Congress,
November 27, 1963

Minutes after President Johnson arrived in Washington, he addressed the nation. His message was simple and brief: "This is a sad time for all people. We have suffered a loss that cannot be weighed. For me it is a deep personal tragedy. I know that the world shares the sorrow that Mrs. Kennedy and her family bear. I will do my best. That is all I can do. I ask for your help—and God's."

He and Lady Bird then went to their home in Washington, D.C. Nineteen-year-old Lynda was a student at the University of Texas, but she joined her parents and her sister, sixteen-year-old Luci (who had recently changed the spelling of her name), in the nation's capital. In December the Johnsons moved to the White House.

To help ease the nation's pain and to ensure a smooth transition, Johnson reached out to many people in the hours and days following the assassination. He called all the living former presidents—Herbert Hoover, Harry Truman,

The Johnsons (left to right: Luci, Lynda, Lady Bird, and Lyndon) moved into the White House in December 1963. President Johnson was often accompanied by his beagles, Him and Her.

and Dwight Eisenhower. Johnson also met with or telephoned other national leaders and President Kennedy's
close aides. He appointed a panel of respected public figures to investigate JFK's assassination. One question was
whether Lee Harvey Oswald—the man who had shot JFK
and who was himself murdered on November 24, 1963—
had acted alone or as part of a larger conspiracy.

President Johnson's priority was to continue with
President Kennedy's plans for the nation. These included a
tax cut and a civil rights bill. Five days after the assassination, President Johnson made a speech to Congress in
which he promised to work toward JFK's goals. He began
by saying, "All I have I would have given gladly not to be
standing here today." Then he said, "No memorial oration
or eulogy could more eloquently honor President Kennedy's
memory than the earliest passage of the civil rights bill for
which he fought so long. We have talked long enough in
this country about equal rights. We have talked for one
hundred years or more. It is now time to write the next
chapter, and to write it in the books of law."

PASSING A CIVIL RIGHTS BILL

The civil rights bill proposed to make race discrimination
and segregation in public facilities illegal. These included
restaurants, motels, libraries, parks, playgrounds, and swimming pools. Under the bill, schools would finally be deseg-
regated, and racial discrimination would be prohibited in
most workplaces.

Many southern legislators opposed the bill when
President Kennedy first proposed it. But Lyndon Johnson
was determined to go down in history as the president who

brought an end to legal race discrimination. He believed that the South would not achieve its full economic potential as long as segregation remained in place.

Johnson also was aware that the effects of segregation went beyond economics. Several weeks after he became president, he hired Gerri (Geraldine) Whittington as one of his secretaries, the first African American person to hold this position. A short time later, he and Lady Bird invited Whittington to swim with them and another guest in the White House pool. "Lyndon was astonished that Gerri Whittington couldn't swim," Lady Bird dictated into her diary that night, "and in his very forthright way, he said, 'What's the matter, couldn't you go to any public pools?' And she, I must say, with very creditable poise, said, 'That is right, so I never learned to swim.'"

Getting the civil rights bill passed took all of Johnson's skills as a persuader and leader. To derail a vote on the bill, southern senators held the longest filibuster in Senate history—fifty-seven days. (A filibuster is a debate that opponents of legislation carry on for a long time to prevent a vote from taking place.)

Johnson had foreseen such a maneuver. He had even warned his friend and mentor, Senator Richard Russell of Georgia, "Dick, I love you and I owe you, but don't get in my way on civil rights or I'll run you down." Russell replied, "Mr. President, you may very well do that, but if you do, you'll lose the election [in 1964] and you'll lose the south forever." Johnson said, "Dick, if that's the price I've got to pay, I'll gladly pay it."

President Johnson did not retreat in the face of the Senate filibuster. He and his supporters finally overcame it,

Upon signing the civil rights bill, Johnson called for Americans to lay aside their differences. He stressed that the bill was proposed by John F. Kennedy, whose brother, Attorney General Robert Kennedy, is at the far left in this photograph.

⸻ ✧ ⸻

and the Civil Rights Act of 1964 passed both houses of Congress in the summer of 1964.

THE WAR ON POVERTY AND THE GREAT SOCIETY

Although President Johnson was committed to JFK's programs, by 1964 he had also started building a presidency of his own. In January 1964, he announced a "war on poverty" in the United States: "Unfortunately, many Americans live on the outskirts of hope—some because of their poverty, and some because of their color, and all too many because of both. Our task is to help replace their despair with opportunity. This administration today, here and now, declares unconditional war on poverty in America." The War on Poverty was waged with the new Office of Economic Opportunity, which trained underprivileged young people for jobs, made loans to small businesses, and gave aid to children and others in need.

LBJ's Civil Rights Journey

Lyndon Johnson was an unlikely champion of civil rights. He was born in the South, and his ancestors fought for the Confederacy (the South) in the Civil War (1861–1865). Like many people of his place and time, he freely used ugly words to refer to African Americans.

Positions he took early in his political career were also unpromising for civil rights. As a congressman, when civil rights bills were proposed, he voted against them. His first speech as a U.S. senator in January 1949 supported the right of his fellow southern senators to engage in tactics to prevent a vote on civil rights legislation.

Yet Johnson showed that he was made of different stuff than many of his southern colleagues. In that same month, January 1949, the funeral home in Three Rivers, Texas, refused the use of its chapel for the burial of a Mexican American soldier. When Johnson heard of this, he said he would help the soldier's family. He did not succeed in getting the funeral director to change his mind, but Johnson arranged to bury the man, Felix Longoria, in Arlington National Cemetery near Washington, D.C. Both Johnson and his wife attended the burial.

By the time he was Senate Majority Leader, Johnson came out more clearly in favor of civil rights. Some critics say that he changed merely for political reasons, so that he would appear to be capable of leading the entire country, not just the South. But many historians disagree, arguing that Johnson's commitment to civil rights reflected his personal beliefs in fairness and equality. James Farmer, a civil rights leader who founded the Congress of Racial Equality, or CORE, said that he had a poor opinion of Johnson before he met with him during Johnson's vice presidency. But Farmer became convinced that Johnson "was not merely working on this [civil rights] because it was politically expedient but because he had a strong belief in it."

As president, Johnson seemed to enjoy surprising the public and challenging white prejudices toward African Americans. In December 1963, he hired a black secretary, Gerri Whittington, to demonstrate his commitment to civil rights. That New Year's Eve, he escorted her to the Forty Acres Club, the segregated faculty club of the University of Texas at Austin. Whittington asked Johnson, "Mr. President, do you know what you're doing?" He replied: "Half of them are going to think you're my wife, and that's just fine with me." To publicize her arrival on his staff, Johnson also arranged to have Whittington appear on the television show *What's My Line?*

Similarly, when Johnson appointed Thurgood Marshall to be the first black solicitor general of the United States in 1965, he wanted to make a splash. (The solicitor general is the government's top courtroom lawyer.) Marshall, who later became the first black Supreme Court justice, said Johnson told him he was giving him the job for two reasons. "One, he thought I could handle it," Marshall said. "Secondly, he wanted people—young people—of both races to come into the Supreme Court Room, as they all do by the hundreds and thousands, and somebody to say, 'Who is that man up there with that swallow tail coat on arguing?' and somebody to say, 'He's the Solicitor General of the United States.' Somebody will say, 'But he's a Negro!' He wanted that image, number one."

Ambitious as the War on Poverty was, President Johnson wanted to do more. In the spring of 1964, he called on the country to build a "great society." His vision was for a society with racial equality, with help for those in need, and with excellence in education. To achieve his goals, President Johnson proposed—and Congress passed—many laws aimed at poverty, health, and education. Medicare, a health insurance plan for the elderly, was one of the first Great Society initiatives. Medicaid, health insurance for poor Americans of any age, soon followed. Under the Great Society legislation, the federal government provided funds for the Head Start preschool program and for elementary and secondary schools. New laws also focused on cleaning up the nation's air and water.

ESCALATION IN VIETNAM

While fighting a War on Poverty at home, the United States faced a military war abroad, in Vietnam. At the time of President Kennedy's assassination, more than 15,000 U.S. military advisers were in Vietnam. These advisers were supposed to support and train South Vietnamese soldiers without engaging in combat themselves. When Lyndon Johnson became president, he was torn about what to do in Vietnam. He did not withdraw from the country, because he subscribed to the "domino theory" and was concerned that all the nations of Southeast Asia would become Communist. But Johnson did not believe that U.S. soldiers could win a war for the South Vietnamese people—they had to fight for their freedom themselves.

Unfortunately, the South Vietnamese government did not command much respect or loyalty from its own people, and its army seemed unable to defend the country against the Communist forces. American soldiers increasingly became involved in the fighting. In a May 1964 conversation with President Johnson, Senator Richard Russell called the situation a "mess" and said he did not know what the solution was. Johnson responded: "That's the way I've been feeling for six months."

The situation soon became messier. In August 1964, a U.S. destroyer ship in the Gulf of Tonkin off the Vietnamese coast reported being attacked by North Vietnamese patrol boats. In response, U.S. planes raided military installations in North Vietnam and Congress passed the Gulf of Tonkin Resolution. The resolution gave the president authority to take all necessary action in Vietnam. It was not a declaration of war, but it was an extraordinary grant of power. Commenting on the extent of the resolution, President Johnson said, "It's like my grandmother's nightshirt. It covers everything."

But Johnson was not eager to use this "nightshirt" to step up fighting in Vietnam. "We are not going to send American boys nine or ten thousand miles away to do what Asian boys ought to be doing for themselves," he said.

THE 1964 PRESIDENTIAL CAMPAIGN

The conduct of the war in Vietnam was a major issue in the 1964 presidential campaign, in which Johnson ran for election as president for the first time. His Republican opponent, Senator Barry Goldwater of Arizona, wanted the United States to take stronger action against Communism. Goldwater even suggested that he might use atomic weapons to destroy Communist supply lines to the Viet

Cong. Many Americans viewed his statement as extremely dangerous. Goldwater coupled his aggressive stance on Vietnam with strong opposition to the increasing role of the federal government in social and economic affairs at home. In addition, he was one of only six Republican senators who did not support the Civil Rights Act of 1964.

Johnson and his vice presidential running mate, Hubert H. Humphrey, a liberal senator from Minnesota, portrayed Goldwater as a dangerous radical. They had many supporters. Democrats mocked Goldwater's campaign slogan, "In your heart, you know he's right," by jeering, "In your guts, you know he's nuts."

———————————————— ✧ ————————————————

The Johnson/Humphrey ticket won the electoral votes of every state except Goldwater's home state, Arizona, and five southern states, where opposition to LBJ's civil rights policies was strong.

Johnson's family did their part to help him win over voters. In October 1964, Lady Bird, Lynda, and Luci campaigned in the South during a "Lady Bird Special" railroad trip. Because many southerners opposed LBJ's actions to promote civil rights for black Americans, the Johnson women did not always get a friendly reception. But they managed to keep up their good humor. When twenty-year-old Lynda heard that a newspaper reporter wrote that she had sung the campaign song, "Hello, Lyndon!" in an "off-key girlish soprano," she joked to her father, "So what, Daddy? That'll just get me the sympathy vote of all those who can't sing on-key."

Election Day in November 1964 brought Johnson a victory that gave new, and true, meaning to his old nickname, "Landslide Lyndon." His forty-three million votes over Goldwater's twenty-seven million marked the largest majority of votes in U.S. history. President Johnson's popularity carried over into Congress as well. Democrats increased their majorities in the Senate and House substantially. Johnson had a mandate from the people for the work he wanted to do to improve American society. He had a friendly majority in Congress to pass the laws necessary to carry out his mandate. And, finally, he had a presidency of his own.

CHAPTER NINE

TRIUMPH AND TRAGEDY

*"I feel like a hitchhiker caught in a hailstorm
on a Texas highway. I can't run. I can't hide.
And I can't make it stop."*

—President Johnson, on the Vietnam War

After his election victory, President Johnson pressed on with his Great Society plans. It was not just the scope of his plans that was ambitious. It was also the sheer quantity of legislation. As one journalist explained, "In the first two full years of his presidency, 1964 and 1965, Johnson submitted and Congress enacted more than two hundred pieces of legislation. Today if a president passes two major bills in a session, it's regarded as a [major success]."

VOTING RIGHTS FOR AFRICAN AMERICANS

A major part of Johnson's plan to build his Great Society was the continued reduction of racial inequalities. Just as people deserved health care, education, food, and decent

Black voters line up at the polls in Alabama. Before the Voting Rights Act was passed, election officials often turned blacks away, telling them that they had come on the wrong day or hadn't followed procedures.

——————————— ✧ ———————————

housing, he felt they also deserved equal rights in society and government. But black people faced serious inequalities. Although the 1964 Civil Rights Act was sweeping and powerful, it had a major gap: voting rights. The law did nothing to ensure that blacks could exercise their right to vote, especially in the South. Johnson and others believed that black people could never achieve true equality if they were denied the right to elect national and local politicians.

Throughout the South, civil rights advocates held demonstrations in support of black voting rights. They met resistance and violence from white mobs and southern government officials. But they had the president of the United States on their side. After Alabama police attacked demonstrators on "Bloody Sunday," Johnson made a historic speech before Congress. On March 15, 1965, he urged Congress to pass a voting rights bill and asked all Americans to take up the cause of African Americans as

their own. He evoked the call of the civil rights movement—"We shall overcome"—and Congress responded
with applause and cheers. The enthusiasm was not unani-
mous, but it was sufficient. On July 9, LBJ signed the
Voting Rights Act of 1965 into law.

RACE RIOTS IN THE CITIES

President Johnson had little time to bask in the glow of his
achievement. Days after he signed the Voting Rights Act,
race riots broke out in a poor black neighborhood of Los

———————— ✧ ————————

*Fires burn in the Los Angeles neighborhood of Watts
during the rioting of 1965. Over the next few years,
similar riots broke out in inner cities across the nation.*

Angeles known as Watts. The violence erupted after a white police officer stopped a car driven by a young black man. In several days of rioting, people looted stores and burned buildings. In the end, thirty-four people were dead, and property damage was estimated at forty million dollars. The riots ended only after twenty-seven thousand police officers and National Guard soldiers enforced order in the streets.

Watts was only the first of many riots. In black neighborhoods in large cities, people who had been too poor for too long were fed up. The promise of the Great Society and voting rights seemed distant to them. In the long, hot summers of 1965, 1966, and 1967, race riots broke out in New York, Chicago, Cleveland, Detroit, Newark, and other cities. More than two hundred people were killed and four thousand were injured. The tremendous efforts made by the leaders of the nonviolent civil rights movement, such as Dr. Martin Luther King Jr., had not gone far enough. America's race problems were far from over.

THE VIETNAM WAR

Vietnam cast an even greater shadow over LBJ's presidency. In 1965 Johnson expanded the U.S. role in the fighting in Southeast Asia. Many of his advisers had warned that South Vietnam was in danger of losing the war, and Johnson did not want to be the president responsible for losing Vietnam to Communism. He ordered U.S. planes to start bombing North Vietnam. American soldiers also attacked targets in South Vietnam that were believed to be Viet Cong strongholds.

Along with the bombing went more American ground troops. No longer were these military advisers on the sidelines.

*Marine helicopters complete a mission in Vietnam. Many Americans,
including Lyndon Johnson, were unsure about U.S. involvement in
Vietnam. But in 1965, the president shook off his doubts and plunged
the United States more deeply into the conflict.*

They were combat soldiers whose job was to fight the Viet
Cong. By the end of 1965, 180,000 U.S. soldiers were in
Vietnam, fighting and dying. In the following years, the
numbers increased dramatically. By 1968, 500,000 American
soldiers were in Vietnam fighting a war that had never been
declared. More than 25,000 Americans were dead.

Johnson's many years of political experience failed him
as he struggled with Vietnam. His negotiating skills did not

succeed in moving North and South Vietnam toward a resolution. For example, he was optimistic that a U.S. offer of one billion dollars for public works would persuade the North Vietnamese to stop fighting. But North Vietnamese leader Ho Chi Minh turned down the offer.

PROTESTS LEFT AND RIGHT

Johnson himself contributed to his problems with Vietnam. Instead of telling Congress and the nation that he planned to expand the United States's role in Vietnam, Johnson proceeded in a more secretive way. He was not forthright about how many American lives his own advisers estimated could be lost in the fighting. As the death toll mounted, many people simply stopped believing Johnson. Race riots were joined by antiwar demonstrations, which sometimes turned violent. "Hey, hey, LBJ, how many kids did you kill today?" was a familiar chant at rallies across the country.

────────────── ✧

Americans who opposed sending U.S. soldiers to fight in Vietnam often organized antiwar protests. College campuses and sites of political events were common locations for demonstrations.

The president's family felt the heat as the turmoil bubbled into a full boil. Protesters seemed always to be marching and chanting outside the White House. "What a house," Lady Bird Johnson wrote in her diary in March 1965, on a day when civil rights demonstrators walked into the White House with tourists and then refused to leave. "What a life."

Both Lynda and Luci lived in the White House. Lynda, who was studious and somewhat shy, had transferred from the University of Texas to George Washington University after her father became president. Luci attended the National Cathedral School and was more outgoing. Although living in the public eye was challenging for the young women, both managed to enjoy friends, parties, and dates. Both also married during their father's presidency. In 1966 Luci married Patrick Nugent, and in 1967 Lynda married Charles S. Robb, a Marine Corps officer in the White House Color Guard.

In January 1966, two-thirds of Americans polled said they supported Johnson's presidency. By October that year, the number was down to 44 percent. And in March 1968, only 26 percent of Americans approved of Johnson's handling of the war in Vietnam. Johnson was criticized both by "doves" who said he was too aggressive in Vietnam, and by "hawks" who believed he was not using enough force to win. Johnson seemed unable to come up with a workable plan for the war. He made decisions but often doubted them. "He had no stomach for it, no heart for it; it wasn't the war he wanted," Lady Bird said. "The one he wanted was on poverty and ignorance and disease, and that was worth putting your life into."

RETREAT

Early in 1968, the Viet Cong and North Vietnamese strongly attacked South Vietnamese cities. The attack, called the Tet offensive, convinced many Americans that the U.S. bombing campaign would not stop the enemy. If the Communists could still launch such a powerful attack after the months and years of bombing, the war was unlikely to end anytime soon.

Vietnam consumed Johnson's presidency. He focused on the war and did not develop new Great Society programs to address many of the urban problems that had sparked the race riots. He did not expand the War on Poverty. War was costly. The country could not support both a war abroad and one at home.

On March 31, 1968, President Johnson appeared on television to give a speech to the nation. He made two stunning announcements. One was that he was pausing most of the U.S. bombing of North Vietnam to seek a peace settlement. The other was that he would not run for the presidency again in the upcoming election in November 1968. Johnson said: "With America's sons in the fields far away, with America's future under challenge right here at home, with our hopes and the world's hopes for peace in the balance every day, I do not believe that I should devote an hour or a day of my time to any personal partisan causes or to any duties other than the awesome duties of this office—the Presidency of your country. Accordingly, I shall not seek, and I will not accept, the nomination of my party for another term as your President."

Some people thought Johnson, who lived and breathed politics, would change his mind. How could he give up the presidency? But he had had enough. "I'm tired," Johnson told a friend after his speech. "I'm tired of feeling rejected by the American people. I'm tired of waking up in the middle of the night worrying about the war."

END OF A PRESIDENCY

Ironically, after announcing that he would not run for reelection, Johnson saw his popularity rise again. But events seemed to conspire to cloud the last months of his presidency. On April 4, 1968, Dr. Martin Luther King Jr. was killed by an assassin's bullet in Memphis, Tennessee. His murder sparked a wave of violence across the country. In 125 cities, rioters set fires, looted stores, and raged in the streets. Forty-five people died. The worst rioting took place in the nation's capital.

Days after Dr. King's death, President Johnson pressed Congress to pass the Fair Housing Act, which aimed to

President Johnson was an ally of Martin Luther King Jr. (left) on civil rights issues, but Dr. King openly criticized Johnson's position on Vietnam.

provide more equal housing opportunities for minorities. When Johnson signed the bill on April 11, he dedicated it to Dr. King. But soon another tragedy gripped the nation: Robert Kennedy, brother of the late president John F. Kennedy, was killed in Los Angeles, California, in early June 1968. Kennedy was running for the Democratic Party's nomination for president, and he had just won the primary election in California. Once again, the nation mourned the death of a Kennedy.

With Robert Kennedy dead, Vice President Hubert Humphrey became the Democratic candidate for the presidency. Humphrey had LBJ's support, but that meant little to many voters, who blamed Johnson for the nation's problems. In the general election in November 1968, Humphrey lost to the Republican candidate, former vice president Richard M. Nixon.

On January 20, 1969, President Johnson and Lady Bird awoke early to have their last breakfast in the White House. Shortly afterward, the Nixons arrived at the White House, and the outgoing and incoming first families drove to the U.S. Capitol. At 12:15 P.M., Richard Nixon was sworn in as the thirty-seventh president of the United States.

The Johnsons flew home to the LBJ Ranch in Texas. After they changed into comfortable clothes, they noticed that their luggage was piled up outside the house. Although Secret Service agents still protected the Johnsons, the bevy of aides who in the past would have carried the bags inside was gone. Lady Bird looked at the luggage and laughed. "The coach has turned back into a pumpkin," she said, "and the mice have all run away."

Johnson retired to Texas with Lady Bird after his lifelong involvement with politics ended in 1969. Throughout his career, Johnson did what he believed was right, even though many of his friends and political allies opposed him.

CHAPTER TEN

LEGACY

"I believe it will be said that we tried."
—President Johnson, on the legacy of
his presidency

Lyndon Johnson was sixty years old when he returned to the Texas Hill Country in January 1969. He had spent his entire adult life in public office. Now he had no campaigns to run, no elections to win, no votes to count. Overnight, his life changed tremendously. He enjoyed playing with his grandchildren. Visiting friends remarked on how Johnson let his gray hair grow long, curling around his ears and neck. Rather than trying to remain active in politics, he turned his attention to the operation of his ranch and business interests. An old Democratic friend said after a visit, "He's become a . . . farmer. I wanted to talk Democratic politics. He talks only hog prices." Johnson also wrote a memoir of his presidency, *The Vantage Point,* which was published in 1971.

Another project Johnson turned to was the building of his presidential library, the Lyndon Baines Johnson Library and Museum at the University of Texas at Austin. The library opened on May 22, 1971. President Nixon visited Austin to accept the library on behalf of the nation. Some uninvited visitors also showed up—two thousand demonstrators protesting the Vietnam War, shouting "No more war" and "Johnson's war" as the ceremonies proceeded.

FADING OUT

A man of sixty might have many years ahead of him, but Lyndon Johnson, like his father before him, was suffering from severe heart disease. In the spring of 1972, Johnson had a serious heart attack. He survived, but he was weaker and sicker than before. He suffered from chest pains and shortness of breath that required him to use a portable oxygen tank from time to time.

The end came on January 22, 1973. Johnson was alone, resting in his bedroom, when he had another massive heart attack. He managed to get to the telephone to call his Secret Service agents, who were nearby. But by the time the agents arrived, Johnson was beyond help.

Ironically, one day after Johnson's death, President Nixon told the nation that the United States had concluded an agreement to end the war in Vietnam. The war that caused Johnson's presidency to unravel would finally come to an end.

CONTROVERSY AND CONTRIBUTIONS

Lyndon Johnson's death did not mark the end of the controversy about the man and his presidency. Debate continues about the Great Society, the War on Poverty, and Vietnam.

Johnson's family enriched the last several years of his life.
Left to right: *Luci, Lady Bird, Johnson's four grandchildren,*
Lynda, and Lyndon at Christmas in 1972.

———————————— ✧ ————————————

Some applaud LBJ's social programs for creating a compassionate and useful government. Others criticize them as examples of big government at its worst and point to the poverty and social problems that still plague the United States after years of government aid. Many Americans see Johnson as responsible for the needless deaths of thousands of American soldiers in Vietnam. Others see him as only one man among many politicians and military leaders who were determined to prevent the spread of Communism.

If Lyndon Johnson achieved nothing else, however, he left a lasting mark on race relations in the United States.

He championed and passed key civil rights laws. He appointed the first African American as solicitor general of the United States and as associate justice of the U.S. Supreme Court, Thurgood Marshall. He appointed the first black Cabinet member, Dr. Robert Weaver, and the first black woman ambassador, Patricia Roberts Harris.

A month before he died, Johnson reflected on his civil rights record. "I'm kind of ashamed of myself that I had six years and couldn't do more than I did," he said. But he had little reason to feel ashamed of his work on civil rights.

——————————— ✧ ———————————

Lyndon Johnson stands in support of Thurgood Marshall (at Johnson's left) as Marshall is sworn in as U.S. solicitor general in August 1965. Marshall's wife and two sons look on at left.

Civil rights leaders Bayard Rustin and A. Philip Randolph wrote, "With the exception of Lincoln, who freed the slaves, no single President contributed as much to the cause of racial equality as did Lyndon Johnson."

Supreme Court Justice Thurgood Marshall went even further. In 1969 he told an interviewer, "I just think Lyndon Johnson, insofar as minorities, civil rights, people in general, the inherent dignity of the individual human being—I don't believe there has ever been a President to equal Lyndon Johnson—bar none!"

TIMELINE

1908   Lyndon Baines Johnson is born on August 27 near Stonewall, Texas.

1924   Johnson graduates from Johnson City High School.

1927   Johnson enrolls in Southwest Texas State Teachers College at San Marcos.

1929   The Great Depression begins in October with the crash of the New York stock market.

1930   Johnson graduates from college and takes a teaching job at Sam Houston High School in Houston, Texas.

1931   Johnson goes to Washington, D.C., to work in the U.S. Congress as secretary to Representative Richard Kleberg.

1933   Franklin Delano Roosevelt becomes president and plans the New Deal to help overcome the Great Depression.

1934   Johnson meets Claudia Alta ("Lady Bird") Taylor. In November Johnson and Lady Bird marry.

1935   President Roosevelt appoints Johnson the Texas director of the National Youth Administration.

1937   Johnson wins election to the U.S. House of Representatives.

1941   Johnson runs for election to the U.S. Senate, but loses to a former governor of Texas, "Pappy" O'Daniel. Japan bombs Pearl Harbor. The United States enters World War II, and Johnson takes a leave from the House of Representatives to serve in the U.S. Navy.

1942   Johnson returns to Congress.

1945   President Roosevelt dies. Harry S. Truman becomes president. World War II ends with the surrender of Germany and Japan.

1948   Johnson wins election to the U.S. Senate.

1951 Democratic senators elect Johnson their party whip.

1953 Johnson becomes Senate Minority Leader.

1955 Johnson becomes the youngest ever Senate Majority Leader.

1957 Johnson helps pass the Civil Rights Act of 1957.

1960 Johnson campaigns to be the Democratic Party's presidential candidate. The Democrats choose Senator John F. Kennedy instead. Johnson becomes his vice presidential running mate. In November, they win the national election.

1963 On November 22, an assassin kills President Kennedy in Dallas, Texas. Lyndon Baines Johnson is sworn in as the new president of the United States.

1964 Congress passes the Civil Rights Act of 1964. Johnson announces a War on Poverty in the United States and calls on Americans to create a Great Society. Congress passes laws to improve the nation's economy, health, and education. Johnson is reelected as president, with Hubert Humphrey as his vice president.

1965 Johnson proposes the Voting Rights Act of 1965, which Congress passes in the summer. Johnson authorizes expansion of the U.S. role in the fighting in Vietnam.

1968 On March 31, Johnson announces that he will not run for reelection as president in November.

1969 President Richard Nixon is inaugurated as president. The Johnsons move back to the LBJ Ranch in Texas.

1973 On January 22, Lyndon Johnson has a massive heart attack and dies at the LBJ Ranch.

SOURCE NOTES

7 Lyndon Baines Johnson, *The Vantage Point: Perspectives of the Presidency, 1963–1969* (New York: Holt, Rinehart & Winston, 1971), 166.

9 Brian D. Sweany, "Voting Rites," *Texas Monthly*, March 2000, 62.

10 Lyndon Baines Johnson, "Special Message to the Congress: The American Promise," March 15, 1965. *Lyndon Baines Johnson Library and Museum,* <http://www.lbjlib.utexas.edu/johnson/archives.hom/speeches.hom/special_messages.asp>.

12 Robert Dallek, *Lone Star Rising: Lyndon Johnson and His Times, 1908–1960* (New York: Oxford University Press, 1991), 41.

12 Jan Jarboe Russell, "Politician of the Century: Lyndon Johnson," *Texas Monthly*, December 1999, 134.

13 Merle Miller, *Lyndon: An Oral Biography* (New York: G. P. Putnam's Sons, 1980), 8.

16 Dallek, *Lone Star Rising*, 35.

17 Robert Caro, *The Years of Lyndon Johnson: The Path to Power* (New York: Vintage Books, 1983), 71.

17 Ibid.

18 Doris Kearns, *Lyndon Johnson and the American Dream* (New York: Harper & Row, 1976), 37.

19 Irwin Unger and Debi Unger, *LBJ: A Life* (New York: John Wiley & Sons, 1999), 19.

20 Dallek, *Lone Star Rising*, 57.

20 "This Is LBJ's Country," *U.S. News & World Report,* December 23, 1963, 60.

21 Miller, *Lyndon: An Oral Biography*, 26.

21 Richard Harwood and Haynes Johnson, *Lyndon* (New York: Praeger Publishers, 1973), 28.

24 Dallek, *Lone Star Rising*, 407.

25 "Simpson's Quotations," *Bartleby.com*, <http://www.bartleby.com/63/51/151.html>.

27 Dallek, *Lone Star Rising*, 79.

29 Ibid., 97.

32 Miller, *Lyndon: An Oral Biography*, 39.

37 "The Presidency," *Time*, November 29, 1963, 21, 33.

37 Jan Jarboe Russell, *Lady Bird: A Biography of Mrs. Johnson* (New York: Scribner, 1999), 93.

37 Miller, *Lyndon: An Oral Biography*, 44.

37 Russell, *Lady Bird*, 105.

38 Robert Caro, *The Years of Lyndon Johnson: Means of Ascent* (New York: Alfred A. Knopf, 1990), 13–14.

41 Dallek, *Lone Star Rising*, 131–32.

43 Ibid., 161.

48 Caro, *The Years of Lyndon Johnson: Means of Ascent*, 219.

51 Ibid., 137–38.

52 Russell, *Lady Bird*, 155.

55 Harwood and Johnson, *Lyndon*, 38.

58 Hubert H. Humphrey, "Oral History Interview II," interview by Michael L. Gillette, 20 June 1977, *Lyndon Baines Johnson Library and Museum,* 2, <http://www.lbjlib.utexas.edu/johnson/archives.hom/biopage.asp>.

59 Ibid.

60 Harwood and Johnson, *Lyndon,* 37.

60 Carl Albert, "Oral History Interview I," interview by Dorothy Pierce McSweeny, 28 April 1969, *Lyndon Baines Johnson Library and Museum,* 14–15, <http://www.lbjlib.utexas.edu/johnson/archives.hom/biopage.asp>.

61 Brian D. Sweany, "LBJ's Living

Legacy," *Texas Monthly*, August 2000, 108.

62 David M. Kennedy, "Lone Star Rising: Lyndon Johnson and His Times," *The Atlantic,* September 1991, 114.

63 William E. Leuchtenburg, "The Old Cowhand from Dixie," *The Atlantic*, December 1992, 92.

64 Patricia and Frederick McKissack, *The Civil Rights Movement in America* (Chicago: Children's Press, 1991), 192.

65 Robert Dallek, *Flawed Giant: Lyndon B. Johnson* (New York: Oxford University Press, 1998), 44.

66 Hugh Sidey, "Boston-Austin Was an Accident," *Time*, July 25, 1988, 23.

67 Miller, *Lyndon: An Oral Biography*, 267.

68 Drew Pearson, "Oral History Interview I," interview by Joe B. Frantz, 10 April 1969, *Lyndon Baines Johnson Library and Museum*, 11, <http://www.lbjlib. utexas.edu/johnson/archives.hom/ biopage.asp>.

70 Ibid.

71 Jim Hargrove, *Lyndon B. Johnson* (Chicago: Children's Press, 1987), 9.

75 Lyndon Baines Johnson, "Address Before a Joint Session of the Congress," November 27, 1963. *Lyndon Baines Johnson Library and Museum*, <http://www.lbjlib. utexas.edu/johnson/archives.hom/ speeches.hom/631127.asp>.

75 Philip Reed Rulon, "Lyndon Baines Johnson," *Discovery Channel School,* original content provided by World Book Online, <http://www.discoveryschool. com/homeworkhelp/worldbook/ atozhistory/j/289700.html>.

77 Johnson, "Address Before a Joint Session of the Congress," November 27, 1963.

78 Michael R. Beschloss, ed., *Taking Charge: The Johnson White House Tapes, 1963–1964* (New York: Simon & Schuster, 1997), 268, n. 6.

78 Sweany, "LBJ's Living Legacy," 108.

79 Lyndon Baines Johnson, "Annual Message to the Congress on the State of the Union," January 8, 1964. *Lyndon Baines Johnson Library and Museum,* <http://www.lbjlib.utexas.edu/ johnson/archives.hom/ speeches.hom/640108.asp>.

80 James Farmer, "Oral History Interview I," interview by Harri Baker, October 1969, *Lyndon Baines Johnson Library and Museum,* <http://www.lbjlib. utexas.edu/johnson/archives.hom/ biopage.asp>.

81 Beschloss, *Taking Charge*, 145, n. 1.

81 Thurgood Marshall, "Oral History Interview I," interview by T. H. Baker, 7 October 1969, *Lyndon Baines Johnson Library and Museum,* 8, <http:// www.lbjlib.utexas.edu/johnson/ archives.hom/biopage.asp>.

83 Beschloss, *Taking Charge*, 369.

83 Public Broadcasting Service, *The American Experience: The Presidents,* "LBJ: Foreign Affairs," <http://www.pbs.org/wgbh/amex/ presidents/frames/featured/ featured.html>.

83 "Lyndon B. Johnson, 1908–1973," *Newsweek*, February 5, 1973, 31, 34.

84 Public Broadcasting Service, *The American President: Lyndon B. Johnson,* "Campaigns and Elections," <http://www. americanpresident.org>.

85 Michael Beschloss, ed., *Reaching for Glory: Lyndon Johnson's Secret White House Tapes, 1964–1965* (New York: Simon & Schuster, 2001), 49.

86 Stanley Karnow, *Vietnam: A History* (New York: Viking Press), 1983, 396.

86 Russell, "Politician of the Century: Lyndon Johnson," 134.

91 "Lyndon Johnson: 1908–1973," *Time,* February 5, 1973, 29.

92 Lady Bird Johnson, *A White House Diary* (New York: Holt, Rinehart and Winston, 1970), 251.

92 Robert Dallek, "Three New Revelations about LBJ," *The Atlantic Online*, April 1998, <http://www.theatlantic.com/issues/98apr/lbj.htm>.

93 Lyndon Baines Johnson, "The President's Address to the Nation Announcing Steps to Limit the War in Vietnam and Reporting His Decision Not to Seek Reelection," March 31, 1968, *Lyndon Baines Johnson Library and Museum,* <http://www.lbjlib.utexas.edu/johnson/archives.hom/speeches.hom/68033.asp>.

94 Simpson, *Contemporary Quotations.* <http://www.bartleby.com/63/50/150.html>.

95 Johnson, *The Vantage Point*, 136.

97 "LBJ As President," *U.S. News & World Report*, February 5, 1973, 72.

97 "Lyndon Johnson: 1908–1973," 29, 33.

100 Lyndon Baines Johnson, "Running Against the Twelfth Man of History," *New York Times,* December 26, 1972, <http://www.nytimes.com/books/98/04/12/specials/johnson-history.html>.

101 Robert D. McFadden, "Nation Is Shocked," *New York Times*, January 23, 1973, <http://www.nytimes.com/books/98/04/12/specials/johnson-shocked.html>.

101 Marshall, "Oral History Interview I," 14–15.

SELECTED BIBLIOGRAPHY

Beschloss, Michael R., ed. *Reaching for Glory: Lyndon Johnson's Secret White House Tapes, 1964–1965.* New York: Simon & Schuster, 2001.

————. *Taking Charge: The Johnson White House Tapes, 1963–1964.* New York: Simon & Schuster, 1997.

Califano, Joseph A. *The Triumph & Tragedy of Lyndon Johnson.* New York: Simon & Schuster, 1991.

Caro, Robert. *The Years of Lyndon Johnson: Means of Ascent.* New York: Alfred A. Knopf, 1990.

————. *The Years of Lyndon Johnson: The Path to Power.* New York: Vintage Books, 1983.

Curtis, Gregory. "Love, War, and LBJ." *Texas Monthly,* November 1997, 9.

Dallek, Robert. *Flawed Giant: Lyndon B. Johnson.* New York: Oxford University Press, 1998.

————. *Lone Star Rising: Lyndon Johnson and His Times, 1908–1960.* New York: Oxford University Press, 1991.

————. "Lyndon B. Johnson Essay." *PBS Online, Character Above All.* <http://www.pbs.org/newshour/character/essays/johnson.html>.

————. "Three New Revelations about LBJ." *The Atlantic Online.* April 1998. <http://www.theatlantic.com/issues/98apr/lbj.htm>.

Dugger, Ronnie. *The Politician: The Life and Times of Lyndon Johnson.* New York: W. W. Norton & Co., 1982.

Goldman, Eric F. *The Tragedy of Lyndon Johnson.* New York: Alfred A. Knopf, 1969.

Goodwin, Doris Kearns. "Lessons of Presidential Leadership." *Leader to Leader,* Summer 1998, The Peter F. Drucker Foundation for Nonprofit Management. <http://www.pfdf.org/leaderbooks/L2L/summer98/goodwin.html>.

————. "109th Landon Lecture." Kansas State University. April 22, 1997. <http://www.mediarelations.kwu.edu/WEB/New/NewsReleases/goodwintext.html>.

Gould, Lewis L. "The Revised LBJ." *The Wilson Quarterly,* Spring 2000, 80.

Hargrove, Jim. *Lyndon B. Johnson: Thirty-Sixth President of the United States.* Chicago: Children's Press, 1987.

Harwood, Richard, and Haynes Johnson. *Lyndon.* New York: Praeger Publishers, 1973.

Johnson, Lady Bird. *A White House Diary.* New York: Holt, Rinehart & Winston, 1970.

Johnson, Lyndon Baines. "Address Before a Joint Session of the Congress," November 27, 1963. *Lyndon Baines Johnson Library and Museum Home Page.* <http://www.lbjlib.utexas.edu/johnson/archives.hom/speeches.hom/631127.htm>.

————. "The President's Address to the Nation Announcing Steps to Limit the War in Vietnam and Reporting His Decision Not to Seek Reelection," March 31, 1968. *Lyndon Baines Johnson Library and Museum Home Page.* <http://www.lbjlib.utexas.edu/johnson/archives.hom/speeches.hom/680331.htm>.

————. *The Vantage Point: Perspectives of the Presidency, 1963–1969.* New York: Holt, Rinehart & Winston, 1971.

Kearns, Doris. *Lyndon Johnson and the American Dream.* New York: Harper & Row, 1976.

Kennedy, David M. "Lone Star Rising: Lyndon Johnson and His Times." *The Atlantic,* September 1991, 114.

Leuchtenburg, William E. "The Old Cowhand from Dixie." *The Atlantic,* December 1992, 92.

"Lyndon Baines Johnson." *The Handbook of Texas Online.* A joint project of the General Libraries at the University of Texas at Austin and the Texas State Historical Association. 1999. <http://www.tsha.utexas.edu/handbook/online/articles/view/JJ/fjo19.html>.

"Lyndon Baines Johnson." *The White House Website.* <http://www.whitehouse.gov/WH/glimpse/presidents/html/lj36.html>.

McKissack, Patricia, and Frederick McKissack. *The Civil Rights Movement in America.* Chicago: Children's Press, 1991.

Miller, Merle. *Lyndon: An Oral Biography.* New York: G. P. Putnam's Sons, 1980.

Newlon, Clarke. *LBJ: The Man from Johnson City.* New York: Dodd, Mead & Company, 1976.

Public Broadcasting Service. *The American President: Lyndon B. Johnson.* <http://www.americanpresident.org>.

Russell, Jan Jarboe. *Lady Bird: A Biography of Mrs. Johnson.* New York: Scribner, 1999.

Sweany, Brian D. "LBJ's Living Legacy." *Texas Monthly,* August 2000, 108.

Unger, Irwin, and Debi Unger. *LBJ: A Life.* New York: John Wiley & Sons, 1999.

FURTHER READING AND WEBSITES

Devaney, John. *Lyndon Baines Johnson: President.* New York: Walker and Company, 1986.

Feldman, Ruth Tenzer. *Thurgood Marshall.* Minneapolis: Lerner Publication Company, 2001.

Galt, Margot Fortunato. *Stop This War! American Protest of the Conflict in Vietnam.* Minneapolis: Lerner Publication Company, 2000.

National Archives and Records Administration. *Lyndon Baines Johnson Library and Museum Home Page.* <http://www.lbjlib.utexas.edu>.

Rubel, David. *Scholastic Encyclopedia of the Presidents and Their Times.* New York: Scholastic, 1997.

INDEX

*Johnson receives a
Lerner book from author
Mary L. Davis.*

ABOUT THE AUTHOR

Debbie Levy's *Lyndon B. Johnson* is her fifth nonfiction book for children. Levy earned a bachelor's degree in government and foreign affairs from the University of Virginia, as well as a law degree and master's degree in world politics from the University of Michigan. She practiced law with a large Washington, D.C., law firm and worked as a newspaper editor. Levy enjoys paddling around in kayaks and canoes and fishing in the Chesapeake Bay region. She lives with her husband and their two sons in Maryland.

◇

PHOTO ACKNOWLEDGMENTS

The images in this book are used with the permission of: The White House, pp. 1, 7, 12, 19, 29, 38, 48, 55, 65, 75, 86, 97; The Everett Collection, pp. 2, 25, 26, 34, 47, 49, 51, 63, 66, 79, 87, 90, 99; © Bettmann/CORBIS, pp. 6, 43, 74, 76, 84, 88, 100; © Flip Schulke/CORBIS, p. 8; Lyndon B. Johnson Library, pp. 13, 14 (both), 16, 18, 22, 36, 40, 61, 69, 96; Library of Congress, p. 31; © Ken O'Brien/CORBIS, p. 33; © CORBIS, pp. 39, 52; Florida State Archives, p. 56; John F. Kennedy Library, p. 73; Records of the Workshop in Nonviolence (WIN), Swarthmore College Peace Collection, p. 91; National Archives, p. 94; © Bettmann/CORBIS, p. 100; Independent Picture Service, p. 111.

Front cover: Lyndon B. Johnson Library